THE BATTLE OF SPION KOP

Livingstone's Lake
The Battle of Majuba Hill
The Rulers of Rhodesia

THE BATTLE
OF SPION KOP

Oliver Ransford

JOHN MURRAY

TO CAROL

First printed 1969
Reprinted 1971

Printed in Great Britain for
John Murray, Albemarle Street, London
by The Camelot Press Ltd., London and
Southampton

7195 1914 4

CONTENTS

ILLUSTRATIONS

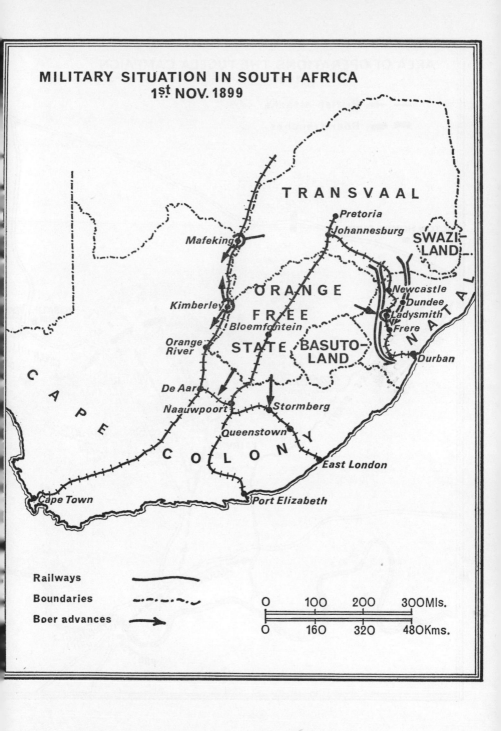

MILITARY SITUATION IN SOUTH AFRICA
1st NOV. 1899

TRANSVAAL

● Pretoria
● Johannesburg

SWAZI-
LAND

Mafeking ●

ORANGE

Newcastle ●
● Dundee
Ladysmith
● Frere

Kimberley ●

FREE

N A T A L

● Bloemfontein

STATE

BASUTO-
LAND

Orange
River

● Durban

De Aar ●

Naauwpoort ●   ● Stormberg

Queenstown ●

C A P E

● East London

C O L O N Y

Cape Town ●

● Port Elizabeth

Railways	————
Boundaries	·—··—··—
Boer advances	→

0   100   200   300 Mls.

0   160   320   480 Kms.

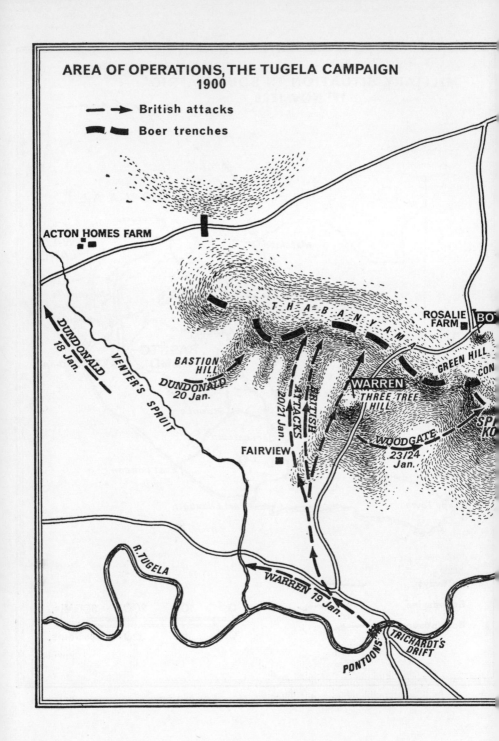

AREA OF OPERATIONS, THE TUGELA CAMPAIGN
1900

➝ British attacks

Boer trenches

ACTON HOMES FARM

THABANYAM

ROSALIE FARM

BO

DUNDONALD
18 Jan.

VENTER'S SPRUIT

BASTION HILL

DUNDONALD
20 Jan.

GREEN HILL

CON

WARREN

THREE TREE HILL

SPI
KO

20/21 Jan.

BRITISH ATTACKS

FAIRVIEW

WOODGATE
23/24 Jan.

R. TUGELA

WARREN 19 Jan.

PONTOONS

TRICHARDT'S DRIFT

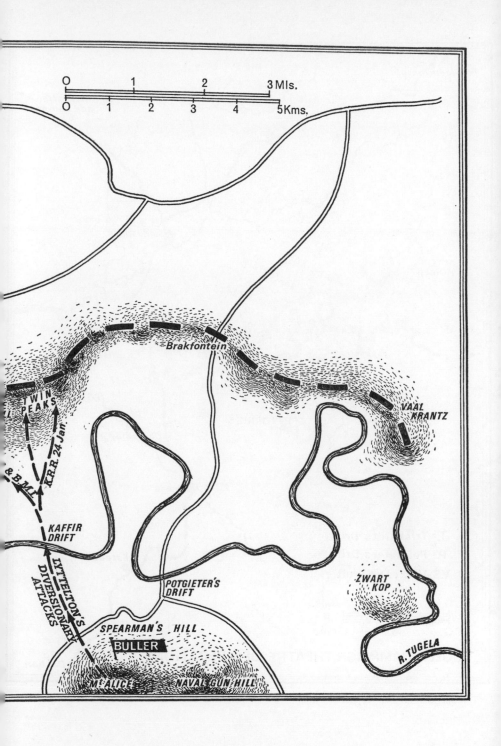

O   1   2   3 Mls.

O   1   2   3   4   5 Kms.

Brakfontein

TWIN
PEAKS

K.R.R. 24 Jan.

VAAL
KRANTZ

& B.M.I.

KAFFIR
DRIFT

LYTTELTON'S
DIVERSIONARY
ATTACKS

POTGIETER'S
DRIFT

ZWART
KOP

SPEARMAN'S HILL

BULLER

Mc ALICE   NAVAL GUN HILL

R. TUGELA

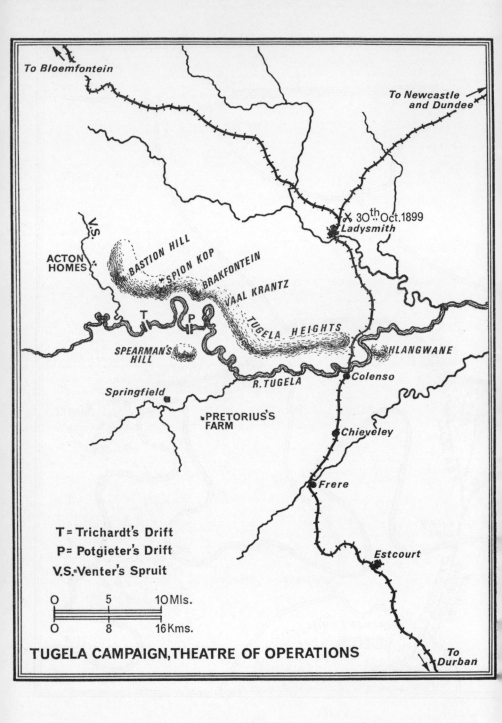

To Bloemfontein

To Newcastle and Dundee

× 30th Oct.1899

Ladysmith

V.S.

ACTON HOMES

BASTION HILL

SPION KOP

BRAKFONTEIN

VAAL KRANTZ

TUGELA HEIGHTS

T

P

HLANGWANE

SPEARMAN'S HILL

Colenso

Springfield

R. TUGELA

PRETORIUS'S FARM

Chieveley

Frere

T = Trichardt's Drift
P = Potgieter's Drift
V.S.= Venter's Spruit

Estcourt

0   5   10 Mls.

0   8   16 Kms.

TUGELA CAMPAIGN, THEATRE OF OPERATIONS

To Durban

ACKNOWLEDGEMENTS

It would be impossible to write a book of this sort without the help of many kind people. To mention them all by name would not be practical, but I cannot forgo recording my indebtedness to the following: Mr. C. J. Barnard, Mr. E. A. Bierman, Mr. A. Colenbrander, Mr. Guillaume de Clerq, Dr. D. J. de Villiers, Mrs. L. de Wet, Mr. B. Downing, Cmdt. G. O. Duxbury, the late Major Edmeades, Mr. M. Fiwella, Miss M. Graham, Mr. A. T. Hadley, Miss Ann Hendrie, Cmdt. L. S. Kruger, Capt. M. N. Lemmer, Mrs. G. Prinsloo, Cmdt. Ploeger, Mrs. C. Rheinallt Jones, Mr. J. Wakelin, Senior Staff Officer, Military & Archival Services, Pretoria, Miss Anna Smith, Dr. R. E. Stevenson, and Mr. George Tatham.

I have drawn on many British and Boer accounts of the battle; these are acknowledged in the bibliography, but I must pay particular tribute to that wonderful monument to scholarship *The Times History of the South African War*. I am grateful to Mr. R. W. Stacey and Mr. N. Johnson, together with their staffs at the two Bulawayo libraries. I owe a particular debt to Mr. Lyonel Capstickdale of the South African Department of Information whose readiness to help I shamelessly exploited.

Once again I must pay especial tribute to my wife who shared all the journeys of investigation and exploration which preceded the writing of this book, and who made them happy.

INTRODUCTION

Near the village of Frere, a third of the way up the trunk road which joins Durban to Johannesburg, the traveller comes to a rise in the ground and sees below a broad and lovely valley through which winds the Tugela river. Beyond the river stands a menacing line of blue hills. As one draws nearer to examine them, these hills sort themselves out into their individual shapes, and one in particular, because of its physical dominance, catches the attention. It is the hill from which the outriders of the Great Trek spied out the promised land of Natal. They called it Spioenkop, the spy hill; today it is better known by the anglicised version of Spion Kop.*

This hill, so peaceful now, was the scene of the bitterest fighting of the Anglo–Boer War of 1899–1902. On its summit was fought the climactic battle of Sir Redvers Buller's campaign to relieve Ladysmith, a campaign which has been stigmatised by a distinguished commentator as a 'display of supreme military incapacity that will find its permanent place in history'.

The battle of Spion Kop is a punctuation mark of history: it marked the end of the Victorian era. It is remarkable for other reasons. One is the uncanny resemblance it bears to the battle of Majuba Hill, fought eighty miles away and nineteen years earlier. Another reason is the impression it gives of still being unfinished; for during its course so many mocking mischances occurred to rob British arms of a brilliant victory, that one is left with the feeling that there is still time for luck to change and allow the struggle to reach a different conclusion.

The story of Spion Kop is the story of 5,000 British soldiers and 600 burghers of the Transvaal and Orange Free State. It is particularly the story of three men: General Sir Redvers Buller, Acting-Commandant-General Louis Botha, and General Sir

* In this book the more common anglicised spelling of Spion Kop will be used.

Charles Warren. It has been told many times by partisans of one side or the other, but rarely comprehensively and objectively.

The story begins in a grimy London railway station one wintry afternoon when General Buller set off to keep his rendezvous with Louis Botha at Spion Kop . . .

BULLER

At exactly twelve minutes past two on the afternoon of 14th October 1899, General Sir Redvers Buller raised a martial finger to his bowler hat and the special train glided out of Waterloo station. He had been given a tremendous send-off; the police experienced difficulty in preventing the cheerful crowd from mobbing the General's carriage, but now as the train gathered speed the temper of the men and women on the platform changed and they broke spontaneously into *Rule Britannia*.

In the roped-off area where the General's carriage had been standing, an imposing array of military gentlemen and Cabinet Ministers were nodding to each other and saluting and standing back for the Prince to leave. For the Prince of Wales himself had come down to see Sir Redvers off. He spent some time in the saloon expressing his conviction that Buller would very soon put things right in South Africa. Then he had taken the General's hand with a gruff 'Good-bye, Buller, good luck to you',[1] stepped on to the platform and the train steamed off.

Few people in England that day would have disagreed with His Royal Highness' opinion that Buller would quickly whip the Boers—least of all the Queen: she was said to think the world of Sir Redvers and only a few days before had been comforted by his calm assurance (whose words must often have returned to haunt him) that he did not expect to have to do much fighting against the Boers, and indeed feared that the war would be over before he even got to South Africa.

It was cold and drizzling when the special train pulled into Southampton later that afternoon, but the City's Mayor was standing there to meet Sir Redvers, and the crowd was just as large as the one in London. The cheers were the loudest that had ever been heard at Southampton docks when the General went on board the *Dunottar Castle* followed at a respectful distance by a little huddle of staff officers, and a group of awed war correspondents (among whom was the twenty-five-year-old Mr. Winston Churchill); one of them reported that when their hero stood for a moment saluting on the gangway 'old men and young men in the throng positively quivered with the emotion, which the most solid and seasoned among them could not but feel'.[1] The crowd was singing the National Anthem as the General went down to his cabin in rare good humour, and when he came on deck again a little later to acknowledge their salutes it was noticed that 'a beneficent smile beamed on the face of the great soldier'.[2] They were still cheering and adjuring Buller to smash the Boers when the *Dunottar Castle* slipped her moorings, and one of the staff officers wrote afterwards of 'a big red-faced Englishman who shouted "remember Majuba" in a strident and penetrating voice, time and time again, until we were out of hearing'.[3] 'He need not have worried,' the officer added, 'we soon had plenty of Majubas of our own.'

It was a fair comment: Buller was setting off to preside over a military campaign which has good claim to be considered the most incompetent ever conducted.

But knowledge of the tribulations to be faced during the next few months were hidden from General Buller that October day. There seemed instead to be every reason for confidence: a whole army corps had mobilised in England during the week without a hitch and he was going to South Africa at the head of the largest and best equipped military expedition that had ever left the country.[4] For Buller had been entrusted with an army that was twice as large as any Marlborough or Wellington had commanded. At this moment 27,000 soldiers were preparing to embark on a veritable fleet of transports, and within the next six weeks they were to be reinforced by 20,000 more men. In addition over 12,000 seasoned troops were already in South Africa and there seemed every reason to believe that Boer opposition to the planned 'steam-roller' march on Pretoria would be very quickly pushed aside. The war, everyone was sure, would be over by Christmas.

Hostilities between Great Britain and the two Boer republics of the Transvaal and the Orange Free State had broken out just three days before Buller climbed on board the *Dunottar Castle*; if anyone had asked him that day why Great Britain had gone to war he would have had no difficulty or hesitation in replying. Nor for that matter would most of his countrymen; the issues seemed perfectly simple to them. Their answers would have run something like this: 'we are fighting to protect our legitimate interests in South Africa and to protect our own kith and kin from oppression by the tyrannous government of President Kruger'. Almost certainly this explanation would have been followed by a long parade of the grievances of their 'kith and kin', and by an angry account of the way these 'uitlanders'* in the Transvaal had been persistently refused the franchise despite the fact that they far outnumbered the burghers of Dutch extraction and paid most of the country's taxes. They had a case there: Kruger in effect had long ago told the uitlanders that if they wished to come and make money in his country they must do so on his terms and without any expectation of being granted political rights. Yet now when time has muted our emotions about the uitlander question it is easy to sympathise with Kruger's attitude: he believed that giving the vote to the uitlanders would lead inevitably to the loss of the Transvaal's independence; 'Do you see that flag,' he once asked a visitor to Pretoria as he pointed to his country's *vierkleur,* 'if I grant the franchise I may as well pull it down.' But towards the end of the nineteenth century British imperial sentiment had been aroused by the victory at Omdurman and the Diamond Jubilee, and the Queen's subjects during these braggart years had come to regard any unsympathetic attitude to their aspirations as something close to impertinence. In particular they refused to tolerate the continued 'persecution' of men and women of their own stock by so feeble a power as Kruger's Transvaal; nor perhaps could they afford to do so, for as Sir Alfred Milner had written in a strongly worded despatch to the Cabinet, 'the spectacle of thousands of British subjects kept permanently in the position of helots, constantly chafing under

* Foreigners.

undoubted grievances, and calling vainly to Her Majesty's Government for redress, does steadily undermine the influence of Great Britain'.

We must remember too that these were days when governments believed they had a duty to protect their subjects whereever they might live, and the mother country had listened to the allegations of ill treatment of Britishers in the Transvaal with increasing anger. Matters had come to a head when an English miner was shot to death by a Boer policeman in circumstances which were generally considered to constitute murder. The killing led to the presentation of an address signed by 20,000 British subjects living in the Transvaal begging the Queen to protect them, and this petition could hardly be ignored by the Government if it was to look for continued loyalty from the British Dominions. The Cabinet responded to it by pressing more aggressively for reform at Pretoria in favour of the uitlanders. This attitude fitted in perfectly with the militant outlook of Mr. Joseph Chamberlain, the Colonial Secretary, and Sir Alfred Milner, the British High Commissioner at the Cape. Both of them had decided that Krugerism must be destroyed before the burgeoning economy of the Transvaal attracted the allegiances of so many white South Africans that it dominated the subcontinent and threatened the British trade routes to the Far East. But at the same time we must remember that a forward policy in South Africa was by no means to the taste of all influential Englishmen; many regarded it as another expression of a growing jingoism which they abhorred; not only did they believe that the uitlanders' grievances were disproportionate to the sufferings which would result from a war, but they said quite openly that these grievances had been deliberately exaggerated by a small group of mining capitalists on the Witwatersrand who were anxious to overthrow Kruger by force for the sake of increased dividends. Imperialism, they protested, had become the plaything of unscrupulous financiers.

And indeed the ambition of a group of speculators did play its part in provoking the war—but it was only one among many

other intertwined factors. Looking back now from the
advantageous position of hindsight, we can see that trouble
was bound to come to South Africa when prodigious amounts
of gold were found in the Transvaal and that country became
flooded with foreign immigrants. For the Transvaal had
suddenly become the most valuable piece of real estate on
earth, and whoever possessed it was bound sooner or later to
dominate the whole of the subcontinent. The only doubt was
whether Great Britain and the uitlanders in particular would be
able to wrest that wealth from Kruger. Commandant-General
Joubert was putting it very well when he said 'there are two
riders but only one horse in the Transvaal. The question is
which rider is going to sit in front—the uitlander or the Boer?'

The British attitude to the Boer republics at the end of the
nineteenth century was conditioned by fear as well as by greed.
Lord Salisbury, for instance, who had hoped to find a peaceful
solution to the problem became convinced that Kruger was
conspiring to eliminate Great Britain's influence from the
whole of South Africa; 'It is impossible to avoid believing', he
wrote to Queen Victoria in the September of 1899, 'that the
Boers really aim at setting up a South African republic, con-
sisting of the Transvaal, the Orange Free State and Your
Majesty's colony. It is impossible to account in any other manner for their rejection of our most moderate proposals.'

Nor were his fears entirely without substance, for a war party
certainly existed in Pretoria; it looked forward to raising
rebellion among the Boers' kinsmen in Cape Colony and
combining to drive out the 'rooineks' from South Africa. 'Our
plan is, with God's help, to take all that is English in South
Africa,' a member of the Transvaal Volksraad wrote about this
time to a friend in the Cape Legislature, 'so, in case you true
Afrikanders wish to throw off the English yoke, now is the
only time to hoist the *vierkleur* in Cape Town. You can rely on
us; we will push through from sea to sea, and wave one flag
over the whole of South Africa under one Afrikander nation if
we can reckon on our Afrikander brethren.'

For sixty years the British and Transvaal governments had

been groping for a way to unite South Africa under a single flag. Admittedly one side wanted that flag to be the Union Jack, and the other the *vierkleur,* but until 1895 there were so many strong cohesive factors at work that they would have eventually effected a compromise solution. After Jameson's wild effort to achieve a *coup d'état* in the Transvaal at the end of 1895, however, a peaceful solution became impossible. For the goodwill and statesmanship which would have averted hostilities were among the victims of the Jameson Raid and from then on an armed confrontation became inevitable. A wave of belligerency affected both sides. When the war came it was welcomed by the large majority of the British people. The Boers entered the war of 1899 with almost equal enthusiasm; the Raid had united the Transvaalers behind President Kruger and had made an ally of the Orange Free State; moreover it had convinced the burghers of both republics that now they would have to fight to preserve their independence and all they held dear. They believed too that they had a good chance of winning the war if they moved before the British were ready, and they cherished the hope that one or two foreign states would intervene on their behalf.

In the war which followed both sides ended up as losers. It seems now to have been one of the most unnecessary ever fought, and it achieved nothing except the consolidation of Afrikanerism. For if Great Britain gained the military victory she failed to achieve her war aims, and the verdict of the war was reversed a little later by the ballot box. Both sides eventually realised the futility of the struggle which had engaged them and Commandant H. F. Prinsloo, one of the heroes of Spion Kop, was speaking for many when he told his son 'it seems a pity that we, belonging to two God-fearing nations, should kill one another like that'. [1]

*

General Buller at sixty was no stranger to war and its dangers: he could look back on a military record that scarcely any contemporary serving soldier rivalled. For Buller had seen forty years of varied army service, and his courage was legendary. He was a big burly man with tiny eyes which usually twinkled with good humour, but his subordinates knew that they could suddenly blaze with an almost uncontrollable temper. A civil servant who worked with Buller summed him up very well when he said he had a rough exterior and an explosive interior.[1] At the best of times Buller's speech was indistinct, since his front teeth had been kicked out by a horse; when angry he became almost incoherent. His face was masklike and his disposition devious. Conan Doyle found him 'a heavy, obdurate, inexplicable man'.[2] Buller, however, was noted for the consideration he showed his servants and he liked to assume the urbane airs of a country squire in public; but when dealing with official matters his manners were brusque to the point of rudeness.

Although the perceptive Ian Hamilton regarded Buller as a 'red faced Martian' devoid of common sense, in 1899 the General had been typed by most of his countrymen as the very embodiment of John Bull. His flaws were generally unknown, for only his intimates realised that his stolid demeanour concealed a distressing lack of self-confidence. Until they were tested during the Boer War his talents, on the other hand, were grossly overestimated. One of Buller's staff officers who had spoken of his chief as 'an impressive, dominating and striking figure' was later to add that 'the curious mixture of obstinacy and vacillation which lay deep down in his nature was concealed from all but a few by his firm, impassive and commanding exterior'.

Buller was a Devonian, born into a large family, and since his mother was a niece of the Duke of Norfolk, his life always rotated in well-connected circles. As a boy he went to Harrow but left hurriedly, 'on account', so his tactful biographer tells us, 'of some difference of opinion with the authorities'.[3] Harrow's loss was Eton's gain, though we learn from the same source that 'his school career does not seem to have been distinguished in a marked way'.[4] He was well known there, however, for his tempestuous temper; on occasion he was heard making valiant efforts to control his tantrums by repeating to himself 'remember Dunmore'—Dunmore being a boy who had once annoyed him during a game of football, and whom he kicked instead of kicking the winning goal. From Eton Buller passed into the army. He was still raw and brash with many small private rages lying not very far below the surface, and his biographer admits that his hero at this time 'had not yet learnt the advisability of keeping his opinions to himself and was rather fond of laying down the law, a habit that does not endear a subaltern to his superiors'.[1]

Yet no one could deny that Buller possessed an unusual brand of courage. It came out in many ways: one was as a horsemaster, for he was a reckless rider with remarkably strong hands; another was the complete unconcern he exhibited when under fire. Buller's military career began in India. Afterwards he went through the China war of 1860 and showed unforeseen strength of character by refusing to wear its medal because he thought the war unjustified.[2] His endurance and dogged leadership during the Red River campaign in Canada soon afterwards brought him to Sir Garnet Wolseley's notice and the promising young officer was admitted into the charmed 'ring' of military cronies which 'England's only General' had gathered about him. About this time Buller inherited a fortune and a fine estate in Devon, and from now on he was placed beyond the need of earning money.

During the Zulu campaign of 1879 Buller proved himself to be a dashing commander of irregular cavalry, and he became known as 'the Bayard of South Africa'.[3] The public doted on this big man who dressed like a buccaneer, and rode into battle with his horse's reins in his mouth, firing a revolver from one hand and swinging a knobkerrie in the other. The great day of Buller's career came at Hlobane on the 28th March 1879 when he rescued several wounded men under fire. He was rewarded with a well deserved V.C., and was promoted into the ranks of British national heroes.

In 1882 Buller again saw service in Egypt and two years later won fresh laurels in a classical example of Victorian heroism when he rallied a broken square during the Suakin campaign. Although Buller made no bones about his opinion of General Gordon, and said that 'the man was not worth the camels',[1] he reluctantly agreed to join Wolseley as his Chief-of-Staff when an expedition was organised to rescue Gordon from Khartoum. It was during this relief expedition that a few percipient colleagues gained their first insight into Buller's vacillating character and dislike of military responsibility: for a superior officer's death precipitated him into the command of an independent column, and he fumbled with it very badly.

But his indecisiveness during the campaign was overlooked in the general recriminations against the Liberal Government following Gordon's death, and Buller was still generally considered to be Britain's most distinguished fighting soldier. Sir Garnet Wolseley was even a little startled to learn that his protégé was 'a veritable god of battle',[2] and someone heard Mr. Gladstone going so far as to assure a friend that 'as a soldier, Joshua couldn't hold a candle to Buller'. Promotion to General followed and Buller was translated to the rarefied atmosphere of the War Office. There he spent the next eleven years moving from one administrative desk to another, and by gaining great influence over the aged Duke of Cambridge, Buller in effect became the Commander-in-Chief of the British army.

In 1898 General Buller's formal appointment to succeed Cambridge was only prevented by a change of government; instead he was given the coveted post of General Officer Commanding at Aldershot. There he impressed his staff by coining a succession of military epigrams: he was forever pointing out that battles are won by resolute bearing in the face of the enemy and he roundly condemned the 'jack-in-the-box' behaviour of soldiers who 'bob up, fire and bob down again';[3] during another exposition on tactics he was heard explaining that 'an attack is like a team of horses: it requires a coachman and if not carefully driven soon gets out of hand.'[4] These maxims were pondered over and remembered but within two years most of Buller's pupils had sadly agreed among themselves that he had quite failed to live up to them.

When he went to Aldershot in 1898 Buller had never commanded more than 2,000 men at a time and his active service had been confined to fighting savages; his energy moreover had been smothered by red tape and his indoor life during the eleven long years at the War Office. He was fifty-nine by now; his talents were only distantly related to the exigencies of modern warfare and he was a little old to learn. Buller knew it; it was gratifying to be regarded as a military wizard, but he realised he was a humbug dressed up as a General and cloaked with old military distinction which hid a nagging loss of confidence in himself. But he had developed a rare capacity to bluff most of his colleagues and his tactical deficiencies were only once exposed during his reign at Aldershot when he was royally out-generalled by his opposite number, the Duke of Connaught, during some well-publicised manœuvres. After this occasion one candid officer was heard to remark that Buller had made 'a superb Major, a mediocre Colonel and an abysmally poor General'.[1] Sir Ian Hamilton later recalled that after the embarrassing field-day Buller 'with a very red face gobbled up all sorts of good things'[2] at a luncheon party and he heard him mumbling disconsolately 'I have been making a fool of myself all day',[3] an admission which was ascribed by most of his listeners to soldierly modesty but by intimates to Grand Mousseaux.

Hamilton went on to confide in his diary that 'I doubt if a man who has been filling his belly with all manner of good things for over ten years in the neighbourhood of Pall Mall can ever quite rise to the rough and tumble of a big command with a formidable enemy'.[4] For by now Sir Redvers' tastes were epicurean and he is rarely mentioned by his contemporaries without some reference to champagne or gastronomy; Cecil Rhodes for instance remarked uncharitably that the General 'only thinks of his cooks and fleshpots'[5] and added that 'he ought to be pensioned'; similarly during the Spion Kop campaign an orderly recorded, 'I sometimes saw Buller . . . in the evening, and as he was a heavy drinker it was obvious to those of us who saw him at close quarters that this was so'.[1] Indeed, in South Africa eyebrows were continuously being raised at the luxury of the great man's quarters, which consisted of a 'superb tent, an iron bathroom, and a sumptuous kitchen with a fine battery of culinary accessories'.[2] Buller confided to one of Queen Victoria's ladies-in-waiting on 18th November 1900 that he 'had had his pint of champagne every day during the campaign, and very good champagne too', adding that his only privation was 'an occasional lack of butter'. But in fairness it must be recorded that if he did do himself very well in the field, few generals have ever been more solicitous of their men's welfare than Buller. Such concern was unusual in the army of Victoria's day and the soldiers responded to it; all through the disastrous Tugela campaign Buller never lost their respect and admiration.

When in the June of 1899 hostilities between Great Britain and the two Boer republics began to appear inevitable, Lord Lansdowne, the Secretary of State for War, sent for Sir Redvers and offered him the supreme command in South Africa. It must be admitted that Lansdowne did this without enthusiasm and, according to Buller, 'in a most ungracious manner'.[3] Buller was equally hesitant about accepting the offer which would so suitably crown his career. He dreaded the prospect of the responsibility which the post carried with it. Directly after his interview with Lansdowne, Buller strode into Wolseley's office and confided to him 'that he was sick of South Africa, and if he was forced to go out he would come away as soon as he could';[4] he was even more explicit in another moment of candour when he told someone else that 'I never credited myself with much ability on the creative side',[5] and he had already surprised Lansdowne by admitting 'I have always considered that I was better as a second in a complex military affair than in chief command'.[6] Lansdowne was inclined after this confession to give Lord Roberts the command in South Africa, but public opinion insisted that Buller was the right man to defeat the Boers and the Cabinet in deference to its voice joined in persuading him to accept the post. And so on 14th October 'the Bayard of South Africa' set out from Waterloo station on his last campaign which would take him to Spion Kop.

Once he was aboard the *Dunottar Castle* Buller literally steamed off into the heaving, lurching limbo of a ship's voyage. There was no wireless telegraphy in 1899, and apart from one stop at Madeira, he was effectively cut off from news for more than a fortnight. As a result the military situation in South Africa as it had been at the time he left Southampton became all the more sharply etched into his mind.

It stared at every him day on board ship when he pored with his staff over the map of South Africa spread out in the converted Ladies' dressing-room which Buller had requisitioned as his office.[1] The map bristled with clusters of little pins representing the Boer commandos which were grouped along the borders of Natal and Cape Colony. Intelligence reports suggested that the Transvaal and Free State had called up 40,000 burghers, but Buller said he knew better and that in his opinion there were twice or even three times that number in the field. The map showed that the Boers were particularly numerous opposite Newcastle in northern Natal and near Kimberley four hundred miles away in Cape Colony. Markers of another colour strung round the enemy republics in a great semicircle represented the British units already in South Africa; they were comfortably clustered together in Natal where Sir George White had 8,000 regulars concentrated at Ladysmith and another 4,000 men under General Penn Symons at Dundee, two hard days' march away. But clearly the British troops were dangerously scattered along the long northern borders of Cape Colony, and it would be nearly three months before all the units of the newly mobilised Army Corps could arrive in South Africa. The staff officers agreed therefore among themselves that Buller might have to improvise a little at first; but they were confident that the Army Corps would have defeated the Boers long before Christmas, and in happy anticipation of its advance they began pushing another set of conquering pins from Cape Town to De Aar, then (a little more slowly) to Bloemfontein, and finally with many flourishes to Pretoria.

For Buller's strategy in the forthcoming campaign was of the ready-made variety. Lord Wolseley and the Cabinet had already decided on the best method of dealing with the two Boer republics and he had inherited their plan. Although they had given serious consideration to advancing into the Transvaal from the firm and loyal base of Natal, this suffered from the disadvantage of having to rely on a single port and railway line; so in the end the Cabinet had resolved that General White must act on the defensive in Natal while Buller's Army Corps directed the main thrust from Cape Colony northwards towards Bloemfontein. The Army Corps would thus be able to utilise three separate ports and three converging railway lines, which allowed of a preliminary concentration at De Aar near the Free State border.

Buller accepted all these arrangements without protest or quibble.

He agreed that White ought to be able to defend Natal for a month or two with the troops at his disposal and that Colonel Kekewich could hold out at Kimberley until Buller had occupied the enemy capitals and won the war. In fact the only contribution General Buller made to the strategic planning of a campaign which was to be fought against the finest mounted troops in the world was a monumental gaffe: he answered loyal offers of help from the colonies with an admonitory 'infantry most, cavalry least serviceable'; [1] the quip of 'infantry preferred' was to pursue him for the remainder of his life.

But Buller was by no means the only officer at the War Office who had misjudged the mettle of the Boers. The British military mind of 1899 was inclined to think of them as rustics who affected the most preposterously ill-fitting clothes (which they strove to conceal by growing vast beards) and who existed almost entirely on a diet of biltong and brandy; one confident journalist even assured his readers that 'the bucolic Dutchman has lost his ancient cunning in wielding his rifle'. [2] Just as they had done before General Sir P. Colley fought his ill-fated Majuba Campaign in 1881, nearly everyone in England believed the burghers to be quite incapable of organised resistance. Indeed a deprecating spokesman at Westminster had been positively apologetic about the way the Government had over-insured victory by mobilising a whole army corps to fight in South Africa. The causes of the earlier defeat at Majuba at the Boers' hands in 1881 had been quite pushed out of British minds, rather in the way the Germans of the 1930's disposed of their own defeat in the Kaiser's War by blaming it on a non-existent stab in the back.

The Boers were in fact a far more formidable body of fighting men than the professional soldiers of Buller's Army Corps. Their forces did not form an army as Europeans knew one: they were collections of men whose ages varied from seventeen to seventy and who had voluntarily enlisted in district commandos under Commandants and Field Cornets of their own choice. These burghers fought in their everyday clothes and from their own horses; most of them had been supplied by their governments with highly effective Mauser rifles which fired magazines of five rounds, but a few were still armed with the older single-shot Martini-Henry gun. Every man among them was a superb marksman and had an instinctive ability to recognise and exploit natural defensive terrain. The Boers may have lacked the formal military training of British troops; indeed they refused to be subject to ordinary discipline but they had been brought up on the military sagas of their race and they had discussed every detail of their forbears' battles; without effort or realisation a thorough knowledge of tactics had been bred into them.

The two Afrikaner republics had spent very large sums of money on munitions immediately before the outbreak of hostilities in 1899, and they were well supplied with artillery. Between them the Transvaal and Free State could muster over a hundred heavy guns of which seventy were modern Krupp and Creusot pieces; they regarded them as mobile artillery rather than as siege guns and performed prodigies in getting

their Creusot 'Long Toms' on to hill positions which professional artillerists would have declared impossible. The Boers
also possessed twenty-two quick-firing Vickers-Maxim guns
which discharged a string of 1 lb. anti-personnel shells: these
guns came as a most unpleasant surprise to the British soldiers
who nicknamed them pom-poms, and although they were not
particularly lethal they were to have a marked effect on morale:
'I have never heard such an extraordinary noise,' wrote one
officer after coming under fire from pom-poms for the first
time, 'seven or eight bangs, a rattle, an amazing clattering and
whistling overhead, then the explosions of the little shells,
which scarred the opposite hillside in a long row of pugs of
brown dust and blue-white smoke, suggesting a lash from a
knotted scourge.'

The men serving these guns—some 800 of the Staats-
Artillerie, and the 1,400 men of the Transvaal police (the
Z.A.R.P.S.)—were the only properly disciplined troops in the
Boer armies, but over 2,000 foreign mercenaries with battle
experience joined them before the outbreak of hostilities. The
ordinary burghers were volunteers who were usually inclined
to accept war as a tiresome civic duty that interfered with their
farming activities, but in 1899 they positively welcomed the
conflict. They were confident that once they had invaded Cape
Colony they could raise rebellion among their kinsmen, and
that they would be strengthened by thousands of Cape
burghers of Dutch extraction. They were sure too that their
God would support them in the struggle.

Time passed slowly for Buller on board the *Dunottar Castle* as
it steamed towards the Cape. He was happy only with his
immediate staff officers and took pains to avoid the war
correspondents in the ship; one of them who had brought a
primitive cinematograph machine on board counted himself
very lucky when he was successful in photographing the great
man on his way to the barber's shop.[1] When the General was
not staring at his map, he spent most of his time absorbed in
Lord Cornwallis's strategical operations during the American
War of Independence which for some reason Sir Redvers

believed bore a marked resemblance to the campaign he was expected to fight in South Africa.[1] His studies, however, were interrupted once by an alarm concerning a Boer privateer which improbable rumour said was steaming to intercept them; on another occasion the General took part in a fancy dress ball, and he found time too to organise a succession of competitions in his capacity as president of the sports committee. There was great excitement one day when the *Dunottar Castle* overhauled a troopship and everyone on board crowded up on deck as the two ships came within hailing distance. Buller was hoping to learn some news about the fighting in South Africa but all that could be made out from the shouting men in the *Nineveh* was an enquiry as to which horse had won the Cesarewitch.[2] But on 29th October they passed a second steamer. It was homeward bound from the Cape, and there was news at last: chalked on a hastily hoisted blackboard they could read 'Boers defeated. Three battles. Penn Symons killed.' Every nuance of this message was considered at length and they were still discussing it next day when the bold outline of Table Mountain stood out from the sea horizon and the seventeen-day voyage was over. Buller landed at Cape Town on 31st October and if he had been starved of news before, now he was overwhelmed by a torrent of military reports, all of which were thoroughly disturbing. The Boers had seized the initiative. They had already clashed three times with White's troops in northern Natal and although the British had claimed three tactical victories, they had ended up with White pulling all his troops back to his base at Ladysmith. On the very day before Buller's disembarkation General White had impetuously attacked the Boers for the fourth time outside that little tin shanty town and, having suffered a sharp defeat, allowed himself to be invested. Natal, as a result, lay open to enemy invasion, and there seemed no reason at all why the commandos should not ride all the way to Durban. Nor was the news from Cape Colony any more reassuring: on the western front Mafeking and Kimberley were both besieged, and although Baden-Powell seemed to be holding his own in Mafeking, Mr. Cecil Rhodes at Kimberley was urging immediate relief lest its garrison be forced to capitulate. The Free Staters were demonstrating in the centre opposite Naauw-poort and Stormberg, and there seemed a very good chance that the British troops there would soon be cut off. Nor was Milner, the British High Commissioner at Cape Town, optimistic about the home front: the whole of Cape Colony, he said, was 'reeking with treachery' and could be expected to break into open rebellion at any moment.

Buller confessed he was 'dazed and dumbfounded' at the way the situation had deteriorated during the seventeen days he had been at sea. One cannot help feeling a little sorry for him. The possibility of rebellion in the Cape had not seriously entered his mind before, and he was heard to mutter that instead of making war on two republics it looked as though he would now have to conquer the whole of South Africa. But Natal was his greatest concern: the few troops there who were not locked up in Ladysmith were strung out in small garrisons along the railway line and appeared to be paralysed by the Boer threat, and on 3rd November, Buller heard that their most advanced units had abandoned the important Tugela river crossing at Colenso. But he fretted too over the threats on the central front to Stormberg and Naauwpoort; a staff officer sent to report on the situation of their garrisons had come back full of confidence that the danger to these places had been exaggerated. Unfortun-ately Buller was unaware of this since the officer had failed to find the Supreme Commander at Headquarters and decided to repair the ravages of a long train journey; while he was thus filling in his time with a hair cut, Buller suddenly lost his nerve and precipitately ordered the two garrisons to withdraw to Queenstown and De Aar. This movement only brought the danger nearer to Cape Town, and as more bad news came in, the General telegraphed a little helplessly to Whitehall about his predicament: 'I landed on 31st October', he said. 'Since that date the situation that has existed can only be described as kaleidoscopic';[1] to his brother he wrote even more dis-consolately that 'I am in the tightest spot I have ever been in'.[2]

All thought of using the Army Corps on a steam-rolling

march to Bloemfontein and Pretoria was abruptly abandoned. As its troops disembarked from their transports they were parcelled off in every direction like so many fingers being stuck into holes in a dyke to stem the Boer flood. Lord Methuen was sent off to the western sector to attempt the immediate relief of Kimberley; General Gatacre was despatched to recapture Stormberg; and General Clery hurriedly embarked with a brigade for Durban to restore the situation in Natal.

It was a bad time for Buller, who sat on and on in Cape Town waiting for more unpleasant news to come in. At least as befitted a Commander-in-Chief he was in a central position from which he could most easily direct and co-ordinate the British armies that were strung out over a vast distance equal to that separating Paris and Vienna. But Sir Redvers chafed at his feeling of impotence, and in the end the strain of waiting became too much for him. On 22nd November he suddenly vanished from Cape Town with two of his staff officers: three days later he turned up in Durban. His prime task, he told reporters there, was to put things right in Natal, by which he meant rallying its scattered troops and effecting the relief of Ladysmith. Not everyone agreed that he had been wise in leaving his central position at Cape Town: Lord Wosleley grumbled that 'he went on his own hook entirely, and at his own instigation. . . . I thought it was wrong,'[1] and Milner was so taken aback by his sudden and unannounced departure that for some time he refused to believe it. Buller tried to silence his critics by explaining that 'I knew what it meant, and that it was doubtful whether we should get through to Ladysmith. I had not the nerve to order a subordinate to do it. I was the big man. I had to go myself.'[2] Those members of his staff whom he had left behind in Cape Town were consoled with an assurance that his absence was only temporary and that he expected to join hands with the Ladysmith garrison in a matter of days rather than weeks. 'We were told he would be back in a fortnight,' one officer remembered, 'and he left much of his kit behind.'[3]

2

BOTHA

While Buller was studying his map in the *Dunottar Castle*, his chief protagonist in the Spion Kop campaign was riding into Natal at the head of a fighting patrol. Louis Botha had been a political opponent of President Kruger and the war party in the Transvaal Volksraad but he unhesitatingly joined the Boer army when he judged that hostilities with Great Britain had become inevitable. 'May the vierkleur soon wave over a free harbour,'[1] he telegraphed to the President at the outbreak and it was clear he already saw that the Transvaal's first objective must be Durban and the outlet to the sea it had sought so long.

Louis Botha in 1899 was a man in his middle thirties, and he possessed a quality given only to the few—the power to influence and move other men. He seemed to know just how much the burghers he was to command during the next two years would stand, and how to get the last ounce of fight out of them. Botha, of mixed Boer and French Huguenot blood, was born a British subject in Natal. His education by modern standards was scanty, but he learned to write a good hand and knew his arithmetic. When Louis was a little boy, chance had led his father to move to a farm in the Orange Free State, but Botha always retained an affection for the British people; indeed his family was divided in its loyalties when war broke out since two of his sisters had married Englishmen and some of his nephews fought on the British side. Although Louis Botha was a stock farmer there was none of the air of the slouchy little farm on the high veld with its dusty roads about him; he was spruce and almost dapper in appearance, his beard was neatly trimmed and he was always well mounted; his interests were not narrow but rather those of a man of the world; yet hidden underneath the restrained appearance was a fighter with a hard instinct for war. But it was his commonsense, his transparent integrity and his charm that most affected all who knew him, and in the Boer army which usually equated military capacity with age, these qualities led to his election as commander-in-chief while still comparatively young.

Like many Boers in 1899, Botha had considerable experience in fighting. As a young man he had joined the commando of Lukas Meyer which in 1884 carved the 'New Republic' out of Zululand, and he had settled down to farming afterwards near its capital, Vryheid. Within a few years the little state was absorbed by the Transvaal and Botha changed his allegiance for the third time. From now on he was a Transvaaler: he was elected to its Volksraad, and when war broke out with Great Britain, Botha was appointed second-in-command of Lukas Meyer's Vryheid Commando. During the first few days of hostilities he led patrols across the Buffalo river into British territory, and he fired some of the earliest shots of the Anglo-Boer War.

It very soon turned out that Botha had a cool aptitude for fighting and was quick to learn tactical lessons from the novel military situation of 1899. His first opportunity to do so came at Talana on 20th October when British soldiers summarily evicted the Vryheiders from a strong hilltop position. Five days later Botha saw action again at Rietfontein, but it was during a third engagement outside Ladysmith on 30th October, the day before Buller landed in Cape Town, that Botha showed convincing evidence of his military genius: Sir George Smith struck out at the Boers who were closing in on the town, and in this crisis Lukas Meyer crumpled up: he withdrew from the battlefield leaving Botha in command. Botha's leadership at once put a ramrod into the back of the Boer defence. They threw the British back and compelled General White to accept investment in Ladysmith.

Botha still had his eyes on Durban; he jokingly told his friends that he wanted 'to eat bananas by the seaside', but his strategical insight told him that the capture of a port would probably lead to intervention by a European power on his people's side. He accordingly insisted that the Boers' proper strategy was to screen Ladysmith with a small number of burghers, while the main force carried the offensive to the coast. But Commandant-General Joubert was a fragile sixty-five, and by nature a timid commander. He saw things in a different way: he preferred to leave the largest part of his army round Ladysmith and would agree to lead only 3,500 Boers southwards across the Tugela river. Even so during November these commandos rode as far as Nottingham Road and they won several skirmishes with the British forces; on one occasion Botha's men ambushed an armoured train and among other prisoners captured Mr. Winston Churchill, who had arrived in Natal a few days earlier to cover the campaign for the *Morning Post*. It was the threat to Durban by Joubert's commandos which convinced General Buller that he must abandon the War Office plan and intervene personally in Natal. By the time Sir Redvers arrived there, however, the scare was over: Joubert had taken a bad fall from his horse a day or two earlier and he was less belligerent than ever. On 24th November the Commandant-General called a council of war, overruled Botha who was strongly in favour of pressing on south, and gave up the Boers' chance of a decisive victory.

Somewhat grudgingly Joubert agreed to hold the line of the Tugela river against the British troops who were bound now to attempt the relief of Ladysmith. He then took himself off to Pretoria to nurse his injuries, leaving Botha behind as his successor with the rank of Assistant-Commandant-General. It was an inspired choice: Botha knew exactly where he should fight the British. By the 27th November he had 8,000 Boers dug in along the hills lining the northern bank of the Tugela astride the railway and overlooking the tiny village of Colenso. There they calmly awaited Buller's attack.

The Tugela river rises in the Drakensberg—the Dragon mountains—and comes tumbling down their cliffs and scarps on to a flat wide valley. For the next sixty miles the river makes its way through this plain in long lazy curves. During this less lively part of its course the river is overlooked from the north by a great roll of foothills projecting from the 'berg'. Their clean

blue shapes form an obtrusive backdrop to the river and frown
like a long line of defiance at travellers approaching them from
the south. The startling clarity of the South African atmosphere
adds altitude to these Tugela Heights, and the clouds they often
foster give mystery to them, so that although few of them rise
more than 2,000 feet above the flats men speak quite naturally
of them as mountains.

These haunted, haunting downs of sandstone, wear a curious
air of expectancy. They have felt history treading over them.
They knew the tiny Bushmen who stalked game across their
slopes; they saw hordes of migrating blackmen seeking homes
for themselves in the fertile riverlands below; they watched the
Voortrekkers on their little ponies riding up to survey the
promised land of Natal from their highest summit—the Spy Hill
or Spioenkop; they caught the sharp note of musketry as
Dingaan's impis attacked the trekkers; and they heard the
sound of British bugles when the infant republic of Natalia was
annexed to the Crown. And now towards the end of 1899 the
Tugela Heights stood waiting for a greater drama in their story
to be enacted.

A few miles below Colenso the Tugela gathers speed again
as it begins to drop down sharply to the sea. Here the river
represents a more formidable military obstacle than in its upper
reaches, and the Boers could reasonably assume that the Ladysmith relief force would make its attempt to cross the river
either immediately to the east of Colenso or somewhere along
the sixty placid miles of its course to the west. Botha's intuition,
however, was more exact: it told him that the attack would be
delivered at the village of Colenso itself, and when it came he
made up his mind to destroy the British army there. He
induced one of his commandos to cross the river and occupy
the isolated hill of Hlangwane on its southern bank. The
remainder of his force he entrenched along the hills which
stand back like an amphitheatre overlooking the river where
a road and rail bridge cross it from Colenso. One of these
bridges was left invitingly intact and Botha gave strict orders
that the Boers were to hold their fire until the soldiers had

advanced across the Tugela. His artillery would then smash the bridge while his riflemen proceeded to destroy the British infantry, who by now would be packed into a perfect killing ground on the northern banks of the river.

Botha had a fortnight to wait for his battle. Buller, who had landed at Durban from Cape Town on 25th November, spent more than a week at Pietermaritzburg tightening up his supply and medical arrangements before moving to the front on 5th December. By now the British troops in Natal had been heavily reinforced; the main camp at Frere made an imposing spectacle and it set an officer in the Naval Brigade writing that he 'had never seen such a fine sight, rows and rows of tents stretching for miles'.[1] Buller received a tremendous welcome at the camp: 'I have never seen troops retempered like this by one man,' wrote a gratified reporter,[2] and one of his colleagues announced that 'General Buller has now arrived at Frere and the matter of the relief of Ladysmith is now well in hand'.[3] It should have been, for Buller now had some 20,000 men at his disposal, the advanced elements of which were at Chieveley where they could watch the Boers beyond the Tugela. It is as well if at this point we pause to describe what they saw and to examine the military problems which faced General Buller if he was to relieve Ladysmith.

From Chieveley the railway line and main road ran down for five miles over an open plain to the Tugela which they crossed at Colenso. On the far side of the river they entered formidable hill country which could be seen extending westwards in a long line towards the distant Drakensberg, while on the east it ended on the southern bank at the isolated hump of Hlangwane. Beyond the hills, they knew, lay the plain in the middle of which stood Ladysmith. Buller's military task involved forcing the Tugela and storming the line of hills beyond. Once his army had debouched on to the plain nothing could stop him reaching this objective.

General White's garrison in Ladysmith that December was known to number rather more than 13,000 soldiers, and in addition some 8,000 civilians were cooped up in the town.

Sickness was rife there and provisions could only be expected to last another month so that the relief force would have to move fast. Buller had no more than a vague idea of the strength of the Boer army opposed to him. We know now that the Ladysmith garrison was contained by a considerably smaller number of Boers under the direct command of Joubert. Botha had another 8,000 burghers entrenched at Colenso, while a few hundred men were spread out along the Upper Tugela watching its drifts. And so although Buller persistently informed Whitehall that the country in front of him was swarming with 80,000 burghers, his army in fact outnumbered the Boers on the Tugela by nearly three to one; and if he could succeed in co-ordinating his movements with those of the Ladysmith garrison he would enjoy an even greater advantage. Unfortunately, Sir Redvers only rarely bothered to inform Ladysmith of his plans, and during the next four months' campaigning, he and White never once exerted their united strengths at a single point.

Joubert maintained that Botha should meet Buller's attack on the line of the Tugela river, but Botha was determined to make his stand in the heights beyond. He explained that this would mean that the British when they attacked him would have to do so uphill, and that he would be able to use the high parapet of the hills to screen his commandos as he moved them from one threatened sector to another; for the Boers were far more mobile than the British with their cumbrous wagon train, and, as Botha wrote, he 'kept his people always on the move, here reducing and there increasing their numbers'.[1]

At first it seemed that Botha's intuition that Buller would attack him at Colenso had been wrong. For following several admittedly casual inspections of the Boer position above Colenso (and particularly after hearing an American military attaché saying dejectedly 'Hell, isn't there a way round?'),[2] General Buller decided that the heights there were impregnable. As he informed the War Office, he then 'did everything in my power to ascertain whether it was possible to get to Ladysmith by any other route'.[3]

There were, as he soon discovered, two other routes by

which he might 'get to Ladysmith'. One lay to the east along a
road passing through Weenen; alternatively he could move his
troops westward and force a crossing of the Tugela at one of
the several drifts above Colenso. But to the nervous Buller
either of these prospects was unpleasing because both meant
leaving the railway line on which he relied to supply his army.
The Weenen road too had the disadvantage of leading through
difficult bush country and it would bring his troops out on the
further side of the hills surrounding Ladysmith. A move up-
river presented a different but thoroughly alarming feature: it
would expose his troops to a dangerous flank attack from the
Tugela Heights while they were strung out in column of march.
In the end, however, Buller decided that this westward approach was the lesser of two evils and on 11th December orders
went out for the army to march on Potgieter's Drift that night,
preparatory to a movement which would turn the enemy's right
flank. Up to this point General White in Ladysmith had learnt
little more about the plans of the relief force than a somewhat
disconsolate message from Buller which read, 'I don't know
which way I shall come,'[1] but once he had decided on his
march to Potgieter's Sir Redvers remembered Ladysmith and
the garrison was gratified to receive a heliograph message to
say that he was shortly leaving for Acton Homes and could be
expected in the town five days later.

On the evening when the relief force was poised to begin its
movement on Potgieter's, Buller was badly shaken to learn that
on the previous day General Gatacre's troops in Cape Colony
had been severely mauled at the end of a night march intended
to regain Stormberg; they had retired in such confusion that a
detachment of 600 men had been left behind to fall into the
enemy's hands. This was bad enough but even more grievous
news came in a little later: Lord Methuen's triumphal advance
on Kimberley had crashed into defeat while he was attempting
a night attack on Magersfontein; his northward advance was
now halted indefinitely.

To Buller's robust intelligence night marches now seemed to
equate themselves with disaster, and he hastily cancelled the

flank movement to Potgieter's scheduled for that evening. His
will to win had abruptly vanished. 'The real fact', he wrote
home dejectedly to a friend, 'is that the enemy have had the
whip hand over us ever since the war began';[1] he told his staff
that all thought of offensive action against the Boers must be
abandoned for the time being; Lord Milner was informed that
'wait a bit is the South African motto and it is the one never
to forget when fighting the Boers';[2] and finally the classical
knowledge of the Officer Commanding at Cape Town was
taxed by the General's advice that 'we have everything to gain
by delay and nothing to lose. All commanders should adopt the
policy of Fabius Cunctator.'[3]

Two days later, however, Buller's mood of pessimism lifted
just as suddenly as it had descended on him, and on the night of
14th December he startled his senior officers with the announce-
ment that he was going to make a frontal attack on Colenso
next morning. Botha's intuition after all had not erred.

The British have always regarded the battle of Colenso, the
third defeat of 'Black Week', as an unmitigated disaster; yet it
was not a disaster on the scale hoped for by Louis Botha; pure
accident prevented Buller's army from falling into the trap that
had been laid for it. This was in no way due to Buller's tactical
insight. He is said to have believed that Hlangwane lay on the
northern bank of the Tugela; at all events he neglected the
obvious course of preceding his attack with the capture of this
hill feature which enfiladed the enemy position. Instead he
simply marched his men in close order across a flat plain towards the Boer trenches above the Tugela, which only a short
time before he had declared to be impregnable. Fortunately
for the soldiers, Botha's plan to annihilate them did not work
out: Colonel Long, the British artillery commander, had some
notion that guns could best be served against an enemy at point
blank range: he therefore galloped his two batteries a mile
ahead of the advancing infantry and opened fire on the Boers
from a distance of only 700 yards. In their excitement the
burghers' instructions to hold their fire until the British troops
had crossed the Tugela were forgotten, and the twelve exposed

guns were overwhelmed by rifle fire. Once they had been silenced the Boer riflemen turned their attention to the infantry which by now was searching fruitlessly for a place to cross the river.

Long's rash action infuriated General Buller, but it sprang Botha's trap and it preserved the British army. A gallant attempt was made by volunteers to save the guns standing forlornly on the plain, and they managed to get two away to the British lines. But many men died in the attempt, and among them was the only son of Lord Roberts, Buller's closest rival in the British military hierarchy of the time. Although he never discussed it in public Roberts in his heart blamed Buller's bad generalship for his son's loss; yet when he came out to South Africa a little later he over-reacted by condoning military blunders which should have led to Buller's replacement, lest it be accounted personal resentment.

Buller astride his big bay horse on the Colenso plain watched the attempt to save the guns in a sort of trance; then suddenly he gave orders for them to be abandoned and for his mangled army to retire to its starting point. Even his closest friends were critical of the way in which he had failed in the crisis: there were plenty of men available to send forward to protect the guns until they could be recovered after nightfall, or at worst Buller could have directed that they be made unserviceable by the removal of their breech blocks. But Buller did neither, and that evening the angry British army watched the Boers gleefully yoking up teams of oxen and dragging the field pieces which represented half its artillery strength back to their own lines together with thirteen wagon loads of ammunition.

What made the defeat at Colenso seem even worse was the fact that it had been lost to an invisible army. Buller's troops had suffered 1,127 casualties without even having had the satisfaction of seeing a live Boer, let alone a dead one. The chances of relieving Ladysmith had now been badly jeopardised and the fault clearly lay with the officer in command. As General Lyttelton, one of the Brigade Commanders, complained later, 'There had been no proper reconnoitring of the ground, no certain information as to any ford by which to cross the river, no proper artillery preparation, no satisfactory targets for artillery, no realisation of the importance of Hlangwane'[1] before the battle, and that 'never has there been a more deplorable tactical display'.[2]

Lyttelton also wrote that 'nothing could be more vague and fluctuating than Buller's estimate throughout the Natal campaign of the number of Boers in the field against him',[3] and now after his defeat at Colenso Sir Redvers tried to soften the blow at home by assuring Whitehall that he had been opposed by 20,000 Boers (it was a number which he was later to double) and he had no compunction in complaining that his 'intentions for the day were frustrated by the actions of my subordinates'.[4] Later on he tried to excuse himself for abandoning his guns by saying that he had been 'frightened by the utter collapse of my infantry',[5] and that 'it was a very trying day . . . it was the hottest day we had the whole of the time we were out there and I had rank bad luck'.[6] But it was neither the heat nor his 'rank bad luck' which had led to defeat; it was due to rank bad generalship and the collapse of Buller's fighting spirit. And that loss nearly precipitated far more serious consequences. For Buller telegraphed home after the battle that 'I do not think I am now strong enough to relieve White . . . my view is that I ought to let Ladysmith go and occupy good positions for the defence of South Natal, and let time help us.'[7] He followed this up with a heliographed message to General White advising him to capitulate, although he added a thoughtful suggestion that he might like to destroy his cyphers and military stores before doing so.

This was something new in British military experience; here was a commanding officer recommending a subordinate to capitulate to a vastly inferior enemy. Perhaps Buller's despair owed something to inebriation, for an onlooker noted of him that 'everything had been going wrong and he sent his despatch to the War Office and then later in the evening when he had had far too much, he sent this message to White'.[8] Fortunately White took no notice of his abject advice.

Stronger nerves than Buller's reigned at the War Office too. The politicians in this crisis turned out to be tougher than the soldiers. Only two members of the Cabinet happened to be in London during the weekend when Buller's telegram came in announcing the defeat at Colenso and his intention to 'let Ladysmith go'. One of them was A. J. Balfour and he immediately sought out his colleague Lord Lansdowne: the two men decided to buttress Buller's resolution with curt instructions that he must either persevere in his attempts to relieve Ladysmith or hand over his command to a subordinate. Next morning the Cabinet met and called upon Lord Roberts to go out and take over the supreme command in South Africa.

'The veritable god of battle' had failed them: 'I can only account for it,' wrote Balfour, 'by the theory that for the last ten years Buller has allowed himself to go downhill, and for the moment at least is not the man he was.' Those nearest to the general formed a similar opinion. Hamilton wrote that, 'Our generalissimo has been so very confident that it was rather a shock to find him in despair after the first encounter';[1] Colonel Sim found Buller the next day 'quite an altered man: the Colenso fight has told on him, so they say, and he has become very quiet and subdued'.[2]

For his part Botha was disappointed that his triumph at Colenso was incomplete, but he telegraphed Pretoria to say 'today the God of our fathers has given us a great victory'. He made an attempt to follow up the success, but his burghers felt they had done enough for one day and they declined to move forward. Many of them went off on leave and the remainder simply lolled about in the sunshine on the banks of the Tugela, and they lost all touch with Buller's army.

From the British point of view the best that can be said about the battle at Colenso is that it revealed the extraordinary courage of the British soldier in appalling circumstances. Looking back at it afterwards Botha said he had been vastly impressed by two things on the 15th December: the ineptitude of the English generals and the gallantry of the men they commanded. Never, he insisted, had he seen human beings rise to such great heights as those who had made their suicidal attempts to rescue Long's guns. 'I was sick with horror,' he told a friend, 'that such bravery should have been so useless.'[1] The ordinary burghers concluded that they were facing an army of lions led by mokes, and their morale rose accordingly.

3

WARREN

On Saturday, 16th December, while the politicians in London were doing their best to inject resolve into General Buller, the third of the principals in the Spion Kop cast was on his way by train from Cape Town to Orange River Station; and he was in a furious temper. General Sir Charles Warren had arrived in South Africa three days earlier. He had come out as commander of the Vth Division and carried instructions to serve immediately under Buller as his second-in-command. Different orders from Whitehall were, however, waiting for him at Cape Town: they told him to supersede the discredited Lord Methuen in command of the Kimberley relief force. On the following day Sir Charles received still more contradictory instructions; he was now to put himself at Methuen's disposal instead of replacing him. It turned out that Buller had prevailed upon the War Office to retain Methuen in command. All these changes were aggravating enough, but Warren's indignation overflowed a few days later at De Aar, 500 miles up the line, after Sir Redvers had been visited by second thoughts: Warren was now instructed to return to Cape Town forthwith and to join the Natal army. For having been persuaded by the Cabinet to make another attempt on Ladysmith, Buller decided that it would be as well to reinforce his troops with the Vth Division, although this unfortunately meant with its commander too. Buller had good reason to be alarmed at the prospect of Sir Charles' close company: Warren was a man noted for his tactlessness and peppery temper; there was a stiff pride about Sir Charles too which made it difficult for him to act in a subordinate capacity; to make things worse, he carried a 'Dormant Commission' to replace General Buller as Commander of British troops in South Africa if for any reason that General was incapacitated or dismissed from his command. For his part Warren was exasperated by the way he had been treated during the few days since his disembarkation: 'I am a shuttle-cock,' he shouted at the unfortunate staff officer who turned him back at De Aar, 'to be ranged about up and down the line.'[1] However, he could do nothing about it but turn his train around, and a week later, on Boxing Day, 1899, he reported with very bad grace at Buller's headquarters in Frere. He and Buller were old acquaintances, and neither of them very much liked what they knew about each other.

Warren in 1899 was in his late fifties. Like Buller he had joined the army as a youth, but his military career had run a rather more unconventional course. His biographer, who was no less eulogistic than Buller's, tells us that at Sandhurst Charlie Warren's 'unusual ability for science and mathematics made it evident that he would have better scope for his talents in the Royal Engineers than in one of the line regiments'.[2] At sixteen accordingly the precocious youth was translated to Woolwich Academy; he emphasised the change of status by acquiring a monocle and always afterwards affected it. Next year, in 1857, Warren received his commission.

After a short course of instruction at Chatham, Lieutenant Warren served in the Engineers for seven years at Gibraltar. He already was beginning to show evidence of a first class, if a trifle unpredictable, brain. At Gibraltar it found expression in a monumental survey of the Rock which won him very favourable notice from his superiors.

After leaving Gibraltar Warren became involved in an unusual interlude: he was given command of an expedition to Palestine which was to elucidate such doubtful questions of biblical archaeology as the course of the Temple Walls and the site of the Holy Sepulchre. This seemed strange employment for a promising young officer but Warren passed the next four years happily enough, exposing ancient walls and, according to his discreet biographer, in even more pleasing activities which were 'more like a continuation of the Arabian Nights entertainment than a record of comparatively modern research'.[3] On one occasion he is known to have startled the Arabs of Jerussalem 'by standing on his head when he excavated and discovered the south-east corner of the 'Temple area',[1] but it seems that in the end they put these acrobatics down to religious fervour rather than to archaeological enthusiasm. Warren stayed in the Holy Land until he was thirty and by then had attained the rare distinction of a sobriquet—he was known to a wide public as 'Jerusalem' Warren.

Warren's archaeological adventures had made him disenchanted with the prospect of a purely military career. 'I was fast drifting into civil life', he wrote afterwards, and was considering 'an appointment as engineer to harbour works in Australia' when he was offered a surprise appointment to survey and delimit the boundary between the Orange Free State and Griqualand West which had just been annexed by Cape Colony. 'Here was the very chance I wanted,' Warren tells us, and in 1876 he began his long association with South Africa.

At Kimberley Warren was caught up in the confused conditions which had followed the discovery of diamonds in Griqualand West. The diamond fields were coveted by the British as well as by the two Boer republics; Warren's task was to reconcile their claims and there is no doubt that he carried it out very well. But the prolonged exhibition of diplomacy was not entirely to his taste and it came as a relief when in 1878 the Gaika War broke out on the other side of the subcontinent and Warren was commissioned to raise a local volunteer unit—the Diamond Fields Horse—to fight in it. It was during this forgotten campaign that Charles Warren first made the acquaintance of Redvers Buller. They were both querulous and irascible men, and it was almost inevitable that they should have quarrelled at their first meeting. But their dislike for each other softened during the years before the Boer War; long afterwards Warren wrote that, 'we often differed very much in opinion on many military and other subjects, but that did not interrupt our good relations, but led to constant argument and chaff'.[2]

In 1882 Charles Warren was propelled into another curious footnote to history—the Palmer Search expedition. A Professor Palmer, sent out on a clandestine mission to win the support of the Sinai Bedouins for Great Britain against Egypt, had disappeared in the desert. Warren's job was to find him. It soon transpired that the professor had been murdered but Warren secured the killers and brought them to justice. It was a creditable performance and the Queen recognised it with a knighthood.

After this success it was natural that Sir Charles Warren should have been considered for the post of leader of the expedition to rescue General Gordon from Khartoum, but perhaps because he announced his intention of getting there through Abyssinia, another commander was chosen. Instead of the Sudan, Warren found himself back in Bechuanaland and charged with the duty of evicting Boer filibusters who had taken over African territories north of Cape Colony. It was a difficult assignment, but Warren got on surprisingly well with the Boers. A settlement was made with Kruger, and Sir Charles presided competently over the inauguration of the Bechuanaland Protectorate. He won some notoriety there too by making a well publicised ascent in a balloon, which set a correspondent of the *Graphic* gushing that it was 'most satisfactory to see what a profound impression of England's greatness these practical and scientific exhibitions have made on the wondering native mind'. It was an exercise which would have been more profitably performed fifteen years later when General Warren fought the battle of Spion Kop without a proper appreciation of the local topography.

Back in England Sir Charles Warren found himself a recognised authority on South African affairs and he tried to profit from his new reputation by becoming a politician. But the General was soundly defeated when he stood for Parliament in the General Election of 1885, and the attempt won him the stern disapproval of Sir Garnet Wolseley who allowed it to be known that Warren could not now expect any military preferment.[1] It seemed that his career in the army was over. Sir Charles *faute de mieux* decided that his proper vocation was that of a savant: he became deeply concerned with the further pursuit of archaeology and in masonic affairs. But in 1886 Sir

Garnet relented, and Warren was sent out to Egypt as Governor of the Red Sea littoral and commander-in-chief at Suakin. He was soon back in London, however, in the rather unexpected role of Commissioner of the Metropolitan Police. His appointment had resulted from a classic blunder by the previous incumbent: in 1886 London was threatened by mob violence, and on 8th February a full-scale riot erupted in Pall Mall; from there the rabble headed north, but a garbled message carried police reinforcements to the Mall instead of Pall Mall, and there they solemnly mounted guard over Buckingham Palace and Marlborough House while the unprotected shops in Oxford Street were looted.

This lapse in staff work had cost the Commissioner his job, and 400 names were hurriedly considered as his successor. Someone suggested 'Jerusalem' Warren, and perhaps because of his success in arresting the murderers of poor Professor Palmer, the post was given to him.

Sir Charles spent an unhappy and undistinguished three years as London's Commissioner of Police. He very soon fell out with the Home Secretary, and then he mishandled an outbreak of rabies during which he was unkindly instructed in the press to 'muzzle yourself as the rabies is in yourself and not in the dogs'.[1] He won applause, however, for his handling of the crowds during Queen Victoria's Golden Jubilee celebrations, but soon afterwards his image was irretrievably tarnished when he called out the Life Guards and Grenadiers to disperse a 'socialist mob' in Trafalgar Square. One hundred and fifty demonstrators were injured during the course of what became known as 'bloody Sunday'. A week later there was another fracas and a man died after being trampled on by a police horse.

Then came the Jack-the-Ripper affair, and all confidence was lost in Sir Charles when time went on and he failed to produce the murderer. Sir Charles had done his best and once he had been seen experimenting in Hyde Park with a pack of bloodhounds, especially brought from Scarborough, to help solve the mystery, but they turned out to be unsuccessful in Whitechapel and the gruesome series of murders continued unabated.

37

It was this failure to end Jack-the-Ripper's reign of terror which finally precipitated Warren's resignation from the Metropolitan Police Force. He is still remembered there, however, for an 'uncontrollable urge to drop into poetry' when drafting his orders; his best known couplet ran: 'The Commissioner has observed there are signs of wear on the Landseer Lions in Trafalgar Square. Unauthorised persons are not to climb on the Landseer lions at any time.'[1]

Sir Charles Warren's career was nothing if not varied: he next served as Officer Commanding troops at the Straits Settlements. His term of office was not a success: 'the tinge of acerbity in the General's temper', one civil servant explained mildly, 'was somewhat conspicuously revealed.'[2] Tact was an impropriety into which Sir Charles rarely lapsed: such great offence did he give to the merchants of Singapore that we read he 'was identified in the public mind with his expensive military policy, and became for a while the most unpopular figure in the Colony'.[3] Nor was it long before his insatiable appetite for an argument caused him to fall out with the Governor, Sir Cecil Smith. It was now too that Warren had his second brush with General Buller, who by this time was installed at Whitehall as Adjutant-General. For Buller had very soon learned to dread the arrival of dispatches from the Straits Settlements which largely consisted of accusations and counter accusations from the incensed pens of Sir Cecil and Sir Charles. 'I am bound to say that you make a good many of the pricks for yourself,' Buller told his military colleague on one occasion and then, warming to his theme, exploded with, 'all I want to say is for heaven's sake leave us alone, do not write and send everything here. . . . I earnestly counsel you to get on better with him if you can.'[4]

In 1894 Warren was back in England and Singapore breathed more easily. Not so the troops of the Thames Command to which he succeeded for the next three years. But Warren was well into his fifties by now; he looked forward to taking things a little more easily, and in the summer of 1898 Sir Charles sent in his papers.

General Louis Botha

General Sir Redvers Buller

Hendrik Frederik Prinsloo

Lieutenant-General Sir Charles Warren

The outbreak of the Anglo-Boer War next year reanimated his restless spirit. He determined to get out to South Africa, although he feared that because he 'had independent views on how to fight the Boers' he might find it difficult to work in harness with the commanders already there. But he thought up an unusual solution: 'Sir George White and Sir Redvers Buller might not subscribe' to his military opinions, he explained afterwards, and 'might even vigorously dissent from them, so I proposed to go out with the St. John Ambulance Brigade.'[1]

Unfortunately for Great Britain's military fortunes, Sir Charles did, however, make a timid enquiry of the Horse Guards as to whether he might be useful in a more active capacity than that of an ambulance driver. Greatly to his surprise, Sir Garnet Wolseley sent for him. There followed a stormy interview, with Wolseley insisting that the best way to deal with the Boers was to edge them out of the entrenched positions which they favoured by a series of flanking movements while his visitor was equally emphatic that better tactical results could be expected 'either by sweeping over them with very long lines of infantry attacking simultaneously' or 'by pounding away at them with artillery till they quailed'.[2]

But despite their disagreement Wolseley offered Warren command of the Vth Division which was being hastily mobilised for service against the Boers, and Sir Charles had a job again and a good one too: he was told he was to go out to South Africa as Buller's second-in-command and succeed him if the Officer Commanding were killed or bowler-hatted.

On 1st December, just before embarkation for the front, General Warren inspected units of his division, and he was as full of confidence as everyone else in the country; according to one eye-witness of the parade 'his parting words were a prediction that the war would be over before we reached South Africa'.[3] Warren's send-off was reminiscent of Buller's. After a triumphant journey which took him through Ramsgate, Broadstairs, Margate and Westgate to Waterloo station, he set off for the front amid deliriously enthusiastic scenes.

On board Warren sternly forbade any relaxation on the part

of his divisional staff. Its luckless officers were either employed
in tedious 'war games' of his own invention which Sir Charles
delighted to umpire, or in listening to their master expound
his strange theory that it was necessary to 'introduce' troops to
their enemies for a few days before allowing the two sides to
come to grips. He would no more lead his men into action
without 'a dress rehearsal', he told the staff, than he would 'take
a team of cricketers who had no experience of football to
compete in a football match'.[1]

Warren landed at Cape Town during 'Black Week', and, as
we have seen, spent the next few days travelling up and down
the De Aar railway line. But at Durban he was gratified to
discover that everyone had lost confidence in 'the Bayard of
South Africa' after the Colenso debacle, and expected him to
put things right; Lyttelton, the most able brigade commander
in the Ladysmith relief force, even went so far as to beg Sir
Charles to hasten north and 'back up Buller, otherwise the
army would go smash'.[2]

The news of Warren's dormant commission to replace him
had touched Buller where he was sore and when 'this dugout
ex-policeman'[3] reported to him towards the end of December
Warren found him tight-lipped and 'rather reserved'.[4] But Sir
Charles was more inclined to ascribe this to shell-shock than to
annoyance and after being surprised 'to find how he had taken
to heart his reverse at Colenso',[5] he somewhat tactlessly let it
be known that in his opinion 'Buller ought to have a month's
rest'.[6]

Nor could Warren refrain from giving Buller a good deal of
jaunty and thoroughly unwelcome advice about how to break
through the Boer lines; Sir Redvers kept his temper for as long
as possible but when the newcomer suggested that the next
operation should begin with the capture of Hlangwane, Dunmore was forgotten and he snapped out 'what do you know
about it?' Warren was so taken aback that he could only reply
feebly 'general knowledge and war games'.[7]

Buller had already been snubbed by the appointment of
Lord Roberts as Supreme Commander in South Africa and

perhaps one can sympathise with his irritation at having this man, who had such an excellent opinion of his own abilities, thrust upon him as second-in-command (and possible successor) of the Natal Field Force. At all events it was now that the idea seems to have germinated in his mind of putting Warren in charge of the next attempt to break through the Boer lines; if it succeeded the overall commander would take the credit; if it failed Warren could be safely left to bear the blame.

4

THE DRESS REHEARSAL

The arrival at the front of Warren's Vth Division brought Buller's army up to 30,000 men, and there was no excuse now for putting off a second attempt to relieve Ladysmith. Sir Redvers pondered over the matter for some time, and, one suspects that because Warren was advocating making an attack below Colenso, he decided instead to revert to his original plan of forcing a crossing of the Tugela at Potgieter's Drift some sixteen miles upsteam.

Warren made it clear that he disliked the idea: he was full of gloomy forebodings about the army being exposed to a flank attack from the Boers hidden behind the Tugela Heights, but he was prepared to qualify this by saying the danger would be lessened if a section of the hills round Doornkop were first seized and held. The suggestion merely drew a sharp rebuff from his chief who said he had no intention of becoming involved in what he termed 'these alpine excursions'.[1]

Sir Redvers was in no hurry to begin the new operation although he was stung by signals from the Boer lines which asked impertinent questions like 'What has Mr. Buller done that Roberts is coming out?'[2] Nor was the General pleased when, in reply to his assurance that Kruger had placed 120,000 fighting men in the field, he received a biting reminder from Lansdowne that the total male population of the Transvaal was barely 90,000.[3] Then early on the morning of 6th January the camp at Frere wakened to the sound of heavy gunfire coming from Ladysmith, and it was clear that the Boers were making an all-out attempt to storm the little town. Heliograph messages asking for assistance kept coming in to his headquarters all morning, but Buller at first seemed disinclined to sanction any move to relieve the pressure. Only in the afternoon did he order a demonstration to be made opposite Colenso: lines of soldiers skirmished up to within a mile of the river, lay down for an hour or so and then leisurely returned to camp. It was all very half-hearted and as the Tugela was in flood and virtually impassable, the Boers did not take these manœuvres seriously. Fortunately the Ladysmith garrison was able to hold its perimeter; but it was a near run thing, and it spurred Buller into action. Orders for the turning movement to outflank the Boers were finalised and issued.

The scheme for shifting his army towards a part of the Boer line which was less strongly defended than the Colenso area was a sound one—provided that the flank march was executed rapidly and the Tugela river and the heights beyond forced without delay. But no idea of taking the Boers by surprise figured in Buller's plan; all he intended to do was to transfer his army with ponderous deliberation from one headquarters at Frere to another at Springfield* sixteen miles away. So slowly in fact did Buller move that the Boers suspected an ulterior purpose at first and regarded the flank march as a feint designed to cover a second attack on Colenso; but after a day or two Botha did take the precaution of increasing the number of burghers watching the drifts on the upper Tugela.

Buller's troops began the march to Springfield on 10th January. Their morale was splendid and one officer thought that this was 'surely the most eager and purposeful army which ever took the field'.[1] Even a bout of bad weather did little to dampen the soldiers' feelings: heavy rain had turned spruits which were insignificant before into torrents and all of them were serious obstacles to the 650 ox-drawn wagons in the column. Even getting the troops from Chieveley and Estcourt to a rendezvous with the main force at Pretorius's farm proved a difficult operation: at one drift the men were obliged to improvise a bridge of wagons over a stream and an onlooker heard them shouting 'what price Westminster Bridge?'[2] as they scrambled across. An awed correspondent described the army as 'wading, sliding, sucking, pumping, gurgling through the mud'[3] but it kept going thanks to the thoughtful provision of ten steam traction engines:[4] these engines looked like modern

* Near present-day Winterton.

43

steam-rollers but they had two small wheels in place of the roller, and they were invaluable in getting the wagon-train through the worst drifts. Warren, the recognised authority on African travel, was at his happiest during the approach march: 'I knew all about the details of putting on extra spans of oxen and hauling on ropes', he wrote later, and he went on to explain complacently that 'I was the only General in Natal intimately acquainted with these matters', and 'turned out in my old capacity as leader or ganger and helped manually'. He added that at first 'I was not recognised, but eventually the men began to know me and look for my help in emergencies'.[1]

Some of his officers felt that Warren could have employed his energies more profitably at the head of the column where he would have been able to take advantage of any opportunities that might arise to surprise the enemy. For by now the Boers had awakened to Buller's intentions and were beginning to move parallel to the centipede crawl of the British army. In Warren's absence it fell to Lord Dundonald commanding the advanced screen of 1,500 horsemen to exercise the only initative displayed during the march.

Moving quickly, Dundonald took the village of Springfield, his first objective, without a fight on 10th January. The country ahead appeared clear of the enemy and Dundonald now decided to exceed his orders and attempt the capture of Spearman's Hill nine miles further on. This hill, some 700 feet high, is made up of two parts known to the soldiers as Mount Alice and Naval Gun Hill. By evening the cavalry brigade was in firm possession of both these important features which commanded the Tugela crossing at Potgieter's Drift.

Next day, 11th January, Dundonald secured this ferry while the infantry trudged gratefully into Springfield. They had completed a gruelling march, and one of their officers wrote with feeling that 'we have come through two or three of the hardest days I have ever been mixed up with'.[2] The advanced troops were then pushed forward to Spearman's Hill which they began to fortify. Their efforts, for a reason that remains obscure, were, however, 'vigorously censured' and 'called folly'[1] by General Buller when he arrived on the scene a little later.

A tremendous view spread out from Spearman's Hill, and Mr. Churchill, whose thoughts were already ranging ahead to the coming battle, gloated over the 'wonderful sight it will be from here' when the fighting began. Spearman's forms one side on an immense basin through which winds the Tugela, curving and doubling back repeatedly on itself like a serpent; it was swollen and brown now from the incessant rains. On the far side of the river the plain stretched away for nearly three miles until it swelled into the blue line of the Tugela Heights. Immediately opposite Spearman's lay a comparatively low section of the Heights called Brakfontein ridge; over it ran a road leading to Ladysmith, whose roof tops could be seen shining in the sunlight seventeen miles away. The town looked enticingly close and officers were laying bets that the siege would be raised within the week. But already this direct route was blocked: the summit of Brakfontein was alive with Boers entrenching and throwing up stone schantzes in what Churchill described as a 'horse shoe position which enclosed the debouches from Potgieter's Drift'.

Buller studied the position with care. It was his custom on these occasions to lie on his back and peer through a telescope which was propped up on his feet. And now he saw that the Brakfontein line was becoming just as strong as the position he had failed to storm a month before at Colenso. So he wriggled round to see what other possibilities there might be of making a break through the Heights. On both sides of Brakfontein were stretched ridges of steep saw-like hills which the Afrikaners call 'ry-kopjes', bound together by narrow saddles or neks. On the east the ridge grew into the stern outline of a craggy hill named Vaal Krantz. On the left lay the even more formidable whale-back hump of Spion Kop, standing out from the Heights like a massive salient. Beyond Spion Kop Buller could see the rolling ridge called Thabanyama, fully three miles long and with its southern face indented by alternating spurs and ravines; Thabanyama appeared to end in a bold promontory which because of its shape the British were already beginning to call Bastion Hill.'* The Tugela Heights angle back northwards at Bastion Hill; seen from Spearman's this stands out against the long line of fortress-like Drakensberg mountains, pearly grey in the far distance.

It did not take very long for Buller to decide that although Brakfontein immediately opposite Potgieter's was practically impregnable, there was a very good chance that Thabanyama might be less strongly held; in any case it looked as though it could be turned from beyond Bastion Hill. Another glance at his admittedly not very accurate map showed that a fair road ran there from the hamlet of Acton Homes through a pass in the Heights and so on to the Ladysmith plain. This road, the General knew, must be an extremely sensitive area to the enemy since it joined the Free Staters' laagers outside Ladysmith with Bloemfontein their capital. A General blessed with quick decisive will power would have sent his troops driving straight for Acton Homes that very morning, but such a quality was missing from Buller's make-up. He was content instead to spend the next few days staring at his maps and the line of hills in front of him, breaking off now and then to discuss with his immediate staff the technicalities of continuing the flank march. Only on the 15th did he send Warren to reconnoitre a ford reported to be four miles up river from Potgieter's. The British called this crossing place Trichardt's Drift; the Boers knew it as Zanddrift. Sir Charles was back later that day to report that Trichardt's was a perfectly feasible place for the army to cross the Tugela. It was accordingly decided that on the following night a flying column would surprise and seize the drift preparatory to beginning a wide turning movement round the Heights. Buller announced that the operation would be conducted by his second-in-command while he himself remained at Spearman's camp with rather less than half his army, poised to take advantage of a Boer retreat by occupying Brakfontein. Warren's flying column was to comprise

* They later named it Childe's Kopje after a well-known officer who was killed on it.

46

15,000 men of the IInd Division plus one Infantry brigade, Dundonald's cavalry brigade, and six batteries of artillery. Buller in effect was now placing the responsibility for the coming operation on to his much vaunted second-in-command, and during the next few days he was happy to adopt the role of a critical umpire. The instructions he gave to Warren were straightforward enough: he was to 'refuse his right' and advance his left wing round Bastion Hill to the Ladysmith plain. General Lyttelton was to mask the initial stages of the movement by demonstrating in force against Brakfontein.

Warren's troops paraded at their camp near Springfield just before six in the evening of 16th January. Elaborate precautions had been taken to conceal their march from the Boers. Tents were left in position on the slopes of Spearman's Hill in full view of the enemy and details remained in the camp to keep ostentatious fires burning and to blow bugles at frequent intervals; the column was to approach Trichardt's at night and along a track screened by hills from the Boers, and absurd stress was laid on the soldiers marching in silence although they were several miles away from the enemy positions.

Everyone who took part in this march by Warren's flying column believed they were setting out on a charmed expedition which embodied all the romance of war. One of the cavalry officers watching the infantry set off, wrote home of the 'miles of stern-looking men marching in fours so quickly that they often had to run to keep up',[1] and Lieutenant Burne of the Naval Brigade found that 'the men in their great coats marching along with the horses and guns mixed up with them reminded me strongly of scenes in pictures of Napoleon's wars'.[2] A medical officer was enthralled with the impression made by 'the Royal artillery, their huge horses, the rattling of their chains, the rumble of the gun wheels, the lances of the cavalry, the nodding cocks feathers in the plumed hats of the South African Light Horse waving in the warm light breeze'.[3] This correspondent tried to capture the atmosphere of a halt on the night march by writing 'a whispered conversation took place between the leaders; dark, mounted figures, silhouetted against the silvery clouds, galloped up and down the ranks, whispering orders to the officers',[1] and he told of how a young bugler boy, 'fresh from Ascot', prepared at one halt to sound the well-known cook-house call but someone had the presence of mind to knock the bugle out of his hand.

At 12.30 a.m. on the 17th the vanguard of Warren's troops reached the hills immediately above Trichardt's Drift. In front of him lay one of the finest opportunities a General could ever hope for: at that moment there were barely 500 burghers guarding the threatened sector of the Tugela Heights and Warren had achieved a concentration of overwhelming force at a decisive point. A direct river crossing here was perfectly feasible to mounted men, and life-lines could have been quickly rigged up to allow the infantry to pass. A rapid push with them that night could hardly have failed to capture the Thabanyama ridge four miles away. Even if Warren had waited until first light a hard gallop by the cavalry could still have seized the Heights and held them until the infantry came up.

But no military force has ever been so inappropriately named as Warren's flying column. It stretched for fifteen miles and took thirteen hours to pass a given point. Nor was it impelled by any sense of urgency. Churchill who accompanied it had already become disillusioned by its commander's dilatoriness and grumbled that 'one main feature has characterised the whole undertaking—its amazing deliberation'.[2]

Certainly on the morning of 17th January Warren had no intention of exploiting his opportunity prematurely: now was the time to demonstrate his maxim that troops fought better if they were given a few days 'introduction' to the enemy. Most of his officers were exasperated by his restraint: one recalled afterwards that 'we all wondered what was the cause of the delay. Some said folly, others incapacity, others even actual laziness',[3] but he tried to console himself with the wry observation that it 'baffled the enemy almost as much as it mystified the troops'.

And so while the British artillery opened a slow bombardment on the scanty enemy field-works in the vicinity, the infantry wasted the golden hours of opportunity on that Wednesday morning in the formalised ritual of throwing two pontoon bridges over the river (an operation which Warren superintended in person) a little upstream from the drift, and in cautiously pushing a brigade across them to hold a bridgehead on its northern bank. No more than desultory firing came from the Boers, and only 'one unfortunate soldier in the Devons was killed' by a sniper in Wright's Farm a few hundred yards away.

The enemy did not waste the breathing space allowed them. Reinforcements were now beginning to hurry to the threatened part of the line opposite Trichardt's Drift, and Botha himself rode up to assume command. He was dog-tired and sickly at the time, and had hoped to get home for a few days' leave. But on the 14th and again a few days later telegrams had reached him from President Kruger: both of them stressed the fact that he was indispensable to the Boer cause and expressed the hope that he would assume command on the upper Tugela. But by now Lukas Meyer had returned to the front, and Botha felt reticent about superseding his old commander as well as the egregious Schalk Burger; yet the President's wishes amounted to a command, and at daybreak on the 18th Louis Botha rode over from Colenso to Thabanyama with 300 horsemen.

Even now it is not difficult to imagine the scene: there stands Louis Botha on the top of Thabanyama beside his lathered white horse, staring at the plain below him and the soldiers moving about over it; one can almost sense his relief when he saw that they were leisurely setting up camp on the northern bank of the river as though they were on peace-time manœuvres instead of fighting a war.

But if there were no immediate danger from the infantry at Trichardt's Drift, Botha soon became aware that another threat was developing in his right flank. For Dundonald by now had shaken himself free from Warren's control and was riding hard with 1,500 cavalry for Acton Homes. They streamed past Bastion Hill without meeting opposition; soon they were cantering on to the direct road from Acton Homes to Ladysmith. Early that afternoon Major Mackenzie with a few troopers encountered a Boer patrol led by Commandant Opperman, and drove it off with heavy casualties. Dundonald then dismounted his men and took up a strong position in the hills above Acton Homes. He was in a winning position and he knew it: the road led on up a gentle slope and could be seen surmounting a pass through the Tugela Heights; the slope was broken up by gullies and small ravines and this would make it easy for troops to work up to its summit under cover. On the far side of the pass Dundonald's map showed that the road entered a broad valley leading to Ladysmith only twenty miles away. If Warren chose to support the cavalry now with infantry and artillery there seemed little to prevent him from enveloping the entire enemy line and relieving Ladysmith.[1]

But Warren refused to follow up Dundonald's success. He said he smelled a trap at Acton Homes, and in any case had no intention of precipitating a general action before he had practised his column in a dress rehearsal. He even went so far as to recall some of Dundonald's cavalry. 'I had to make certain,' he explained afterwards, 'that the mounted troops did not in the exuberance of their zeal get themselves into positions where they could not be extricated.'[2] What Sir Charles was in fact trying to say was that he did not regard his cavalry brigade as a fighting unit but rather as a screen to protect his infantry; and he was nervous, he always was, of a devastating Boer counter-attack.

Even if this counter-attack failed, it might still succeed in stampeding his trek oxen while out grazing and so immobilise his column, and the thought preyed on his mind. Next day Warren's concern had increased rather than lessened and he caused Dundonald still further distress by giving categorical orders that the bulk of his brigade was to come back to the bridgehead. 'There are no cavalry round the camp,' Warren explained in his message, 'and nothing to prevent the cattle being swept away.'[3] As Dundonald bleakly notes in his autobiography, 'this order paralysed the mounted brigade at the very moment when it needed strengthening'.[4] Warren by now had reduced Dundonald's command to a mere 800 men and he could relax: he had arranged things as he had wanted them, and he was heard to mutter that his cavalry commander 'could go to the devil and do what he liked with the rest of his horsemen'.[1]

No one in the British army had got round yet to realising that if the Boers were given two days to construct field-works, it was next to impossible to turn the burghers out of them, and the 18th January was allowed to pass peacefully at Trichardt's while the soldiers consolidated their bridge-head only slightly harassed by desultory rifle fire from the Boers who were perfecting their defences on Thabanyama. There was only activity at Potgieter's where Lyttelton made another demonstration against Brakfontein, using a captive balloon to observe the effects of 600 rounds of gun fire.[2] More grumbling was heard about Warren's lack of activity, but Sir Charles said he was very pleased with the way things were going and it seems he communicated some of his optimism to his officers, for we find Lieutenant Burne noting in his diary that, 'all our army experts are surprised, and I think we must have caught them (the Boers) on the hop, as they don't reply to our artillery fire'.[3]

On the 19th Warren decided that his troops had become sufficiently familiar with the Boers to allow him to begin feeling his way round the enemy flank and he got them on the move again. But even now the march was not pressed. 'Anything more deliberate than Sir Charles Warren's movements,' the disgruntled Birdwood wrote home, 'I have never seen.'[4] The sun admittedly was fiery that day, it was hard going through country broken up by innumerable dongas, and the commissariat arrangements were faulty: 'Fearfully hot day,' one regimental record runs, 'nothing to eat, but rum and biscuits served out at 8 a.m.' There was a good deal of confusion when the head of the long column came up to Venter's Spruit but Warren at least enjoyed this additional opportunity to demonstrate his handiness with a wagon train. Dundonald, who had come back in person to plead for reinforcements, found the General 'taking an active part with his voice in urging the drivers to do their best' at the crossing; he was dismayed by a repetition of Warren's refusal to support his horsemen and puzzled by the General's explanation that: 'Our objective is not Ladysmith; our objective is to effect a junction with Sir R. Buller's force and then await orders from him.' One feels it was as well that Dundonald did not discover that a little earlier General Warren had held back the Mounted Brigade's wagons at the drift with the comment that 'if I let them through Lord Dundonald will try to go on to Ladysmith'.[1]

If Warren had really intended to turn the Boer flank that Friday morning, he very soon lost heart: when he had got half his column across Venter's Spruit, he suddenly decided that it was particularly vulnerable to an enemy swoop from the hills, and that afternoon he brought the troops back close to their old camp at Trichardt's.

By this time two thousand burghers were entrenched on Thabanyama, and they watched the British column's clumsy movements below with attention and interest. President Steyn of the Free State had paid them a morale-raising visit that day. General Buller had likewise paid his flying column a visit. He did not conceal his impatience at the way Warren had been manœuvring for three days on the upper Tugela without getting to grips with the Boers. Warren was full of explanations and excuses, but at the end of a rather unpleasant interview he had not succeeded in impressing Buller. Indeed, Sir Redvers seriously considered removing his second-in-command from control of the operations.[2] 'On the 19th I ought to have assumed command myself,' Buller wrote later. 'I saw that things were not going well—indeed everyone saw that,'[3] and he added contritely, 'I blame myself for not having done so'.

Yet Buller's visit did goad Warren into calling a conference of his senior officers that same evening. He dealt briskly with the problems facing them: there were two ways, he said, of reaching Ladysmith: they could either go by Acton Homes, or they could take a more direct track over Thabanyama that passed through two farms called Fairview and Rosalie. Warren went on to say that he did not particularly like the Acton

Homes route as it would dangerously lengthen his line of communication; it would be better, he thought, to attack along the shorter Rosalie road but only after softening up the Boer positions astride it by prolonged artillery bombardment. What he was suggesting of course was to make a frontal assault on a prepared position instead of following his instructions to turn the enemy flank, but his commanders agreed with him, and so it was arranged. He was probably a little apprehensive about Buller's reaction to the change of plans, for the message he sent him about them showed more than his usual penchant for obfuscation: 'I am going to adopt some special arrangements,' he signalled Spearman's Camp, 'which will involve my staying at Venter's Spruit for two or three days.'[1]

Warren put in his long-delayed attack on Thabanyama before it was light on Saturday, 20th January, supporting it with an elaborately contrived flanking fire. The infantry skirmished forward in long lines towards a spur projecting from the main ridge called Three Tree Hill. It came as something of an anti-climax when their objective was found to be unoccupied, and was taken without loss. Presently, however, the attack was resumed against the real Boer position.

An understanding of the shape of the Thabanyama ridge is fundamental to the comprehension of the fighting which followed during the next two days. The ridge swells out of the Tugela plain, presenting an easy slope to the south which looks rather like that of downland country in England. From the summit of Thabanyama, however, the ground drops down far more sharply to the Ladysmith plain. Several spurs project from the southern face of the ridge, and they reminded one officer who fought there of the fingers of a hand whose wrist was the main mass of Thabanyama.[2] The Boers had made their trenches in two semicircular lines along the rolled crest of the ridge; behind it the sharp descent provided ideal cover for their ponies which they providently kept saddled in case a retreat became necessary. Their trenches faced on to a grassy glacis, fully a thousand yards across and quite devoid of cover.

The next British attack went straight up the third and fourth 'fingers' projecting from the Thabanyama ridge, and so on to the glacis. The choice of terrain was unfortunate: a far better opportunity awaited Warren had he extended his attack to the left, for by now his artillery barrage had driven the Boers out of the trenches on the western half of Thabanyama. But Warren can scarcely be blamed for being ignorant of this development: three Boer scouts—Slegtkamp, Hindon, and De Roos—had covered it up by reoccupying the trenches, hoisting a *vierkleur,* and maintaining a rapid rifle fire from them. Their stratagem was effective: thirty-six British guns opened up again on what was considered to be a strongly held position. The three scouts' ordeal lasted several hours: Slegtkamp wrote afterwards that he buried his head in the ground on the ostrich's principle that if he could see nothing, no one could see him.[1]

The British troops made their attack on Thabanyama in the old style, led by a Brigadier-General waving a naked sword in his hand. The soldiers had been trained to charge their enemies in this manner, accepting the necessary casualties until they could get in among them with the bayonet. This had worked very well in the past when fighting savages, but it did not work at all across open ground against an enemy as brave as themselves and armed with automatic rifles; the attacks simply stalled six hundred or more yards short of the Boer trenches. The troops showed great gallantry but they were not used to South African conditions and they were particularly affected by the heat. 'All day long,' one of them wrote afterwards, 'we worked and fought under a hot shell and rifle fire without food or water.'[2] By afternoon the flying column was halted and had succumbed to a feeling of hopeless stalemate.

Yet now, in a haphazard sort of way, the fates suddenly gave Warren another opportunity to win the Natal campaign with a single blow: Dundonald, on his own again, came riding back to the sound of guns from Acton Homes; as he passed under Bastion Hill he could see Boer riflemen on the ridge beyond enfilading the British infantry attacking up the slopes of Thabanyama. Hoping to reduce the pressure he detached a handful of dismounted men to clamber up Bastion Hill. The

The crossing at Trichardt's Drift

Summit of Spion Kop looking across to Aloe Knoll and
Twin Peaks

Summit of Spion Kop looking across to Conical Hill
(British trench-grave in middle foreground)

few burghers nearby were too intent on the main attack to prevent Dundonald's men from effecting a secure lodgement on the crest of the hill. Without support the troopers could go no further, but they had provided Warren with another splendid chance to roll up the entire Boer position.

But exploitation on his left flank still did not fit in with his tactical plans and Warren studiously ignored Dundonald's toe-hold on Bastion Hill. Instead, the attack on the eastern end of Thabanyama was resumed next morning after a vigorous bombardment by six field batteries. What followed was as pointless as the previous day's fighting: despite severe casualties the soldiers found it quite impossible to reach the Boer trenches, and the feeling grew stronger among them that they were being used to no good purpose. Like another prophet descending from his distant Sinai, Buller rode over again from Spearman's that Sunday morning to see how Warren was getting on. He indulged himself for some time in criticising the dispositions of the troops and them ambled off alone on his horse to see what was happening at Bastion Hill. 'I concluded that he was trying a little warfare on his own',[1] Warren explained later, and indeed Buller did so far forget his self-imposed role of testy umpire as to direct a two-battalion attack along the crest of Bastion Hill. But by now the Boers were prepared and the attack failed; Buller then returned to Spearman's, avoiding what would have been an embarrassing second call at Three Tree Hill, and Warren politely forbore to probe 'the mystery' of the way he had spent the morning.

We must remember that trench warfare was quite new to the British army in 1900, and that its officers had failed to learn the lessons of the American Civil War. Yet despite all the mistakes that had been made they were nearer breaking through the Boer lines on Thabanyama that Sunday afternoon than Warren imagined. For the burghers had been shelled now for several consecutive days and they had not taken to it kindly when the British artillery was strengthened by four howitzers. Some of the Boers began to drift away from the firing line. A German officer serving with them wrote: 'I see now our people are coming away from the position. It is almost enfiladed by the howitzers which simply blow away the entrenchments. All is lost if the British make an assault now. There is not a man in the trenches.'[1] A doctor in the Boer lines similarly noted in his diary: 'Our men are beginning to get very jumpy and nervous, as their trenches are lying mostly in open rolling country and according to many of the burghers could be rushed'; another of his entries says, 'the strain of the continuous fighting is beginning to tell on the burghers', and it went on, 'if things continue like this for a few days longer, the Boers will break and run'.[2]

It was not only the continual shelling and the strain of wondering when the British would find a sensitive spot in their line which had shaken the Boers: their commissariat had broken down too; the commandos on Thabanyama were desperately short of food and had to make do with rusks and the few buck they were able to shoot; medical supplies had also run out, and the burghers were going down one after the other with dysentery contracted from drinking infected water. It was only Botha's resolution which held the Tugela Heights line together. He was to be seen everywhere, riding from one position to another, supporting his men's will to resist with his own sturdy self-confidence, listening to their complaints, and exhorting them to go on fighting. It was a gruelling time for him: 'I am exhausted,' he admitted to a friend, 'with complaining and talking to get them back in position.'

All this, however, was unknown to Warren and he called off the attack when it was on the verge of success. Next morning, Monday the 22nd January, Buller rode over as usual to Three Tree Hill to see how the operations were progressing. He was in one of his blustering moods and when he found the front quiet again he made no secret of his dissatisfaction. The meeting between the two men was more strained than ever, and Buller threatened to replace Warren if the situation was allowed to drift any further. He wrote later: 'I said that he must either attack or I should withdraw his force. I advocated as I had previously done an advance from his left.' There is a fatuity about the conversation that followed which still has the power to irritate us. Warren was sufficiently startled by Buller's threats to promise another attack on Thabanyama, although he thought two more days should be used for softening up the position with shell fire. At the same time he firmly rejected the idea of advancing from Bastion Hill: 'If successful,' he told Buller, 'it would mean taking the whole line of the enemy's position which they might not be able to hold.'[1] Not surprisingly this ludicrous answer only served to make Buller still more angry. The two men's accounts of what followed are discrepant, but it seems that an evil fate made Warren mutter that anyway it was impossible to get up the Fairview road without taking Spion Kop first. Buller replied irritably: 'Of course you must take Spion Kop.'[2] It had become difficult for the two men to agree about anything during the last week, but here now was something on which they concurred, although their agreement had been reached in the most casual of fashions. Warren privately believed that Sir Redvers replied so sharply because 'he had evidently not thought the matter out',[3] but the damage was done and in this haphazard sort of way a decision was made to attack Spion Kop that very night. Buller very soon regretted that he had assented to this operation. 'I did not like the proposal,' he wrote later, and recalled that he tried to put Warren off by 'saying that I always dreaded mountains, but after considerable discussion I agreed to his suggestion'.[4] He says too that once back at Spearman's Camp he went so far as to draft a letter to say that he would have much preferred the offensive to be resumed on the left flank[5] but then decided to let Warren have his own way.

Warren's account of the meeting merely states that on second thoughts he said he favoured the attack being made on Green Hill and then only after a thorough artillery preparation, but this did not meet with Buller's approval, and that 'rather than retire'[6] he promised to attack Spion Kop that night; he further arranged for the operation to be carried out by Major General Talbot Coke's Lancashire Brigade. Buller could at least feel satisfied that he had prodded Warren into some sort of activity, and one can imagine him sitting down to his dinner that night confident that the deadlock would now be broken. But even now he did not know Warren's capacity for procrastination.

As soon as he had heard of the Spion Kop scheme General Coke said that he would like a day to reconnoitre the hill's approaches and that anyway his troops were too tired to go into action that night. Warren jumped at the chance this gave him of postponing the attack for twenty-four hours, but he unfortunately forgot to notify Buller of the delay. Coke for his part strolled off to his nearby camp through the darkness, promptly lost himself in the veld and had to spend the night out in the open. It was clear that finding his way about in the dark was not General Coke's forte; it was to have disastrous consequences two nights later.

Buller rode over to Three Tree Hill early next morning expecting to find that Spion Kop had been seized during the night and the Boer line breached; he was furious to discover instead that nothing had been done at all, and he was only slightly mollified by a firm promise that the attack was planned for that very night, Tuesday, 23rd January. Yet even now Buller could not refrain from favouring Warren with a morsel of advice: perhaps because he was angry with Coke he said he had his doubts about that General's staying-power in view of a lame leg and 'desired that the assault column be led by the more energetic General Woodgate.'[1] Coke, he added, should assume command of the Vth division, while Warren, the overall commander, would have to make do with a small improvised staff for the operation. But Buller knew that he was going to have his battle at last; at Spearman's that evening he sent a telegram home which caused great excitement in London: it read: 'An attempt will be made tonight to seize Spion Kop the salient which forms the left of the enemy's position.'[2] There could be no going back now. The 'dress rehearsal' was over.

5

ASCENT

The grassy plateau of Thabanyama ends on the east in a well-marked promontory which was named Green Hill by the soldiers during the Tugela campaign. From Green Hill the ground dips down very steeply into a gully and then reaches up again to the commanding ridge of Spion Kop. Spion Kop is nearly three miles long and is divided into two halves by a narrow connecting saddle. The part nearest Green Hill is hog-backed and its shape reminded a journalist with Buller's army of Arthur's Seat near Edinburgh.[1] The humped top is absolutely bare of trees, but its slopes are furrowed by dongas and scored with boulders, and among them little groups of trees have found precarious holds. The southern face of the hill is a sheer drop: 'Its precipitous sides,' idly commented a watcher on Spearman's, 'show white glistening spots in the morning sun—quartz strata.'[2]

From Warren's camp at Three Tree Hill a broad spur could be seen running out from the south-western part of Spion Kop, and this clearly offered a reasonably easy ascent to the summit. The spur is marked by three successive step-like ledges. The lowest ledge, about half way up the spur is heart-shaped and comparatively extensive. The intermediate step adjoins the hill's southern cliffs and is no more than a narrow ledge. The highest shelf is much larger and is still marked, as one poetical officer noted during the battle, by a 'half-dozen or more dwarf but bushy mimosa trees, now covered in yellow button blossoms, sweetening the air with their perfume'.[3]

The eastern half of Spion Kop, which is the more elevated of the two, cannot be seen from Three Tree Hill. Warren must have had plenty of opportunity to study it during his column's crossing of the Tugela at Trichardt's Drift, but during the battle on Spion Kop which followed he seems to have forgotten its existence. The summit of this part of the hill is marked by three sharply defined conical peaks, only two of which can be seen from the south so that the British called this part of the ridge 'Twin Peaks', while the Boers referred to it as 'Drieling Kopje'—Triplet Hill. It must be emphasised again that so far as Warren and his officers were concerned Twin Peaks did not exist. They considered only the nearer hump-shaped section of Spion Kop to be their objective, and indeed the entire extent of the hill. Buller from his post on Spearman's Hill on the other hand had a far better conception of the true shape of Spion Kop, and during the coming battle when he referred to its summit he was speaking of its entire three-mile stretch which included Twin Peaks. This was a factor which was to cause a great deal of confusion.

If his perception of the extent of Spion Kop was erroneous, Warren knew nothing at all about the configuration of its summit. Lacking an up-to-date map he seems to have assumed it to be a ridge like Thabanyama but with a lengthy field of fire towards the north, and this impression appeared to be confirmed by the long line of a second spur he could see extending northwards, which ended after a thousand yards in a cone-shaped knoll. Little effort seems to have been made to question any local Africans about the shape of the summit, and the farmer on whose land Spion Kop stood had fled to Ladysmith and was unavailable.

In fact the western half of Spion Kop is a three-cornered 'table mountain' whose top is shaped roughly like an isosceles triangle with angles pointing north, south-west, and east-south-east. The southern face of the triangle measures 450 yards, the western face 420 yards, while the north-eastern face is the shortest of the three, measuring 400 yards. Boulders are scattered about the summit in little groups with coarse grass growing between them, and are particularly numerous along the line of the north-eastern crest which they serrate like a natural battlement. The hill top is not perfectly flat, rather it is gently dome-shaped with the highest part lying roughly in the centre of the plateau. Each of its angles is pulled out as it were into spurs so that all the faces of the hill appear concave from below. The south-western spur points towards Tric-hardt's Drift. The northern spur is the one that Warren had seen ending in a conical kopje before dropping steeply into the Ladysmith plain. The easterly spur forms the saddle-backed ridge, invisible from Three Tree Hill, which as we have seen broadens out after about a mile into the narrow plateau bearing the Twin Peaks. There is one feature of this connecting ridge which was to be of decisive importance during the battle: the saddle is interrupted a quarter of the way along by a small elevation on which many spiky aloes grow: it was to gain unenviable fame as Aloe Knoll or (in Afrikaans) Alwyn Kopje.

From their vantage point on Three Tree Hill Warren and Woodgate could no more see Aloe Knoll than Twin Peaks and consequently had no idea that it commanded the apparently dome-shaped objective they had set themselves. It was a lack of knowledge which could of course have been remedied by the most elementary patrol activity, but Warren limited his recon-naissance to a cursory inspection of the south-west spur by which he intended his troops to ascend Spion Kop. Of all the many mistakes which he made during the Tugela campaign this failure to recognise the existence of Aloe Knoll was probably the most reprehensible; out of it came tragedy, for without possession of this feature the remainder of Spion Kop is practically untenable.

We must pause for a moment here to consider how strategi-cally important was the capture of Spion Kop, and this brings us at once to the essential weakness of the plan which Buller and Warren had so casually adopted. For the seizure of Spion Kop alone could have had little result: its capture would only be significant if the attack on it had been part of a larger scheme which would drive a wide hole into the Boer line. But neither Buller nor Warren seems to have intended the Spion Kop operation to be anything more than an isolated thrust involving only a single brigade. They did not consider following up the capture of the Kop by widening the scope of the offensive, although this would have been made easy since troops dug in on the summit of Spion Kop would have been able to enfilade the Boer trenches on Thabanyama, and most military authorities maintained that with artillery on the summit, those trenches would not have been tenable for more than an hour. (It is only fair, however, to point out that this opinion was not unanimous and some artillery officers insisted that guns could not be fought from so exposed a position.) The generals in short had set themselves a limited objective: they hoped to break into the Boer line, but they had given no thought to breaking through it. Warren seems to have cherished a vague hope that the hill's loss would make the Boers panic and abandon the whole line of the Tugela. One doubts whether Buller's lucid discernment had reached even so definite a conclusion: when asked by a staff officer what Woodgate's force should do after it had captured the summit, he cogitated over the problem for some time, and then grunted, 'It has got to stay there'.[1]

We can see now that if it was to be carried out, the capture of Spion Kop should have been regarded not as a narrow operation but rather as a lever with which to wrench open the enemy line. This could have been effected if Warren's scheme had envisaged hauling guns to the summit the moment it was captured, but here one touches on perhaps the most tragic lapse in the British planning. For although there was a pale intention to get artillery up to the plateau after its seizure, no one made certain that the proper guns would be available.

The most suitable guns for the purpose were those of a mountain battery attached to Buller's army; these guns could be taken to pieces for transport on pack mules, so there would have been little difficulty in getting them up Spion Kop. Unfortunately they had been left behind at Frere when the troops moved to Springfield a fortnight earlier and no one had thought of bringing them to the front since then. Nor had they been remembered on the day when the Spion Kop operation was decided upon. In the casual and haphazard manner which characterises the operations of the Ladysmith relief force it was only next morning—the 23rd January—that the mountain battery was belatedly remembered and a message was sent to get it up to Trichardt's Drift without delay. This, however, still allowed time for the guns to be carried up the Kop behind the assault column—but unaccountably the vital message failed to reach Frere. There was some consternation at Three Tree Hill when the battery did not arrive, and Colonel à Court, who had been seconded to General Woodgate from Buller's staff as liaison officer, was inclined to delay the march until it came up, 'but', he explains lamely, 'we could not wait for it'.[1]

Warren assigned the task of capturing Spion Kop to Major-General Talbot Coke's Lancashire Brigade. As we have seen, at the last moment Buller arranged for Coke to be replaced by Major-General Woodgate whom he considered more active. Warren disliked this decision and by altering the command structure of the Brigade it was indeed responsible for a good deal of the confusion which followed. Later on he succeeded in restoring Coke as task force commander but by an ironical twist this only served to make the confusion much worse.

Woodgate's assault column of 1,700 men was drawn from the Second Battalion Lancashire Fusiliers, the Second Battalion the Royal Lancaster Regiment (The King's Own), two companies of the First Battalion the South Lancashire Regiment, together with a half company of Royal Engineers and two hundred men of Thorneycroft's Mounted Infantry, an uitlander unit which had been recruited in Johannesburg and Natal and which was dismounted for the operation.

The Task Force assembled at dusk on Tuesday, 23rd January, in a gully behind Tree Tree Hill. It was a warm cloudy evening. The men hung about as their officers fussed around with nominal rolls, and presently they were called to attention for Woodgate to address them on the importance of moving quietly and avoiding smoking during the climb.

It was 8.20 p.m. and dark before the column started off on the six-mile approach march to Spion Kop. At first the men moved quite rapidly in column of fours along a well-marked track that crossed the broad valley separating the base of Spion Kop from Green Hill but later the country became rougher and broken up by water courses and progress was delayed.

General Coke stood beside the road to see them off and a little further on there was a large heap of sandbags: it had been intended that each soldier should carry one sandbag up the hill, but since the pattern of the coming operation was already becoming established as one in which something was always going wrong, nobody remembered to give the necessary order and the sandbags which could have alleviated the coming disaster were left behind, a forlorn little pile standing in the valley.

The column reached the base of Spion Kop at about midnight. There was a brief rest while the officers searched in vain for a section of water carriers who had failed to put in an appearance; then the ascent proper began. Led by Thorneycroft's Mounted Infantry the troops were moving now in single file up a zigzag goat path which was lined by boulders. It was drizzling and the men found conditions very eerie as they climbed up the hillside. For the most part they moved silently, and all that could be heard was the thin swish of boots through the wet grass, an occasional shot from Thabanyama where British pickets were still in contact with the enemy, the clink of rifles against side arms and canteens, the hooting of an owl, and the muttered oaths when a man tripped against a covered stone. The night was pitch black; only one light was to be seen far below—the distant glimmer of a single hurricane lamp which hung from Warren's wagon on Three Tree Hill. The hushed column was led by Colonel Thorneycroft, and it would have been difficult to find a better leader. Thorneycroft at this time was a few days short of his fortieth birthday. He was a giant of a man, weighing well over twenty stone, who had a knack for leadership and a driving pugnacity. Lord Birdwood, then a subaltern, was not alone in considering him to be 'one of the most outstanding officers of those days'.[1] Thorneycroft was supposed to be assisted during the climb by two African guides who knew the hill, but one of them ran away at the first opportunity and the other was so terrified that he was of no use at all, and the Colonel had to rely therefore on his instinct to find the path in the darkness. Behind him came

64

à Court and General Woodgate. Woodgate was elderly, and he had to be helped up the steeper parts of the slope by his companion. The men were tired before they began the ascent, and some of them dozed stupidly beside the path when halts were ordered on the successive shoulders of the hill. The slope between was very steep and sometimes they were obliged to clamber up on all fours. There were numerous delays as officers rounded up stragglers and all accounts mention the great concern that was occasioned by a white spaniel dog which frisked around the column; someone eventually got a lead round his neck and led him back to camp before it alarmed the picket of Boers on the summit.[1] All these diversions added up to delay: it takes a fit man a little more than an hour of daylight to get up Spion Kop but in the darkness and confusion of a tiring night march the troops took four and a half hours to make the ascent.

They were not the only men moving on Spion Kop that night. A group of burghers was struggling and sweating and cursing in an attempt to get a heavy gun up its northern slope and on to the summit. Two days earlier Botha had thought it might be a good idea to have a field-piece there to shell Warren's bridges at Trichardt's Drift. He deputed Commandant Prinsloo to see whether this was practicable. Prinsloo on this occasion was dilatory: he delayed a day before making his reconnaissance, yet by the strange logic of events this turned out to be a stroke of luck for the Boers, for if the British had captured a cannon and ammunition on the summit of Spion Kop, the outcome of the battle would almost certainly have been different. It was not until the early morning of the 23rd that Prinsloo climbed the hill; he returned a little later to report that it would be difficult but possible to get a 76 mm. Krupp gun on to the summit. A section of German engineers serving with the Boers was immediately sent up to prepare an emplacement for it, while another detachment brought a Krupp cannon up to the base of the hill, and as soon as it was dark began hauling it up the slope. Once emplaced on the summit, the Boer command believed, their situation would be immensely strengthened: 'If only the enemy gives us tonight,' General Schalk Burger telegraphed about the project to Joubert's headquarters near Ladysmith, 'then we trust with God's help to hold the position.' He had no idea that 'the enemy' were not giving them 'tonight'.

Apart from the Germans digging the gun emplacement, there were 70 burghers of Commandant Solomon Grobler's Vryheid commando on the summit of Spion Kop that night. This small number was considered to be perfectly adequate for its defence in view of the steepness of its slopes. During the past two days the Vryheiders had hacked out two shallow trenches at the top of its south-western spur and when the light failed on the evening of the 23rd, half the burghers spread out their blankets to sleep while the remainder manned the trenches. They did not think it necessary to push out any pickets in front of them, and no one heard the approaching soldiers until they were almost on top of them. 'The sentries must have sadly neglected their duty,' writes a contemporary Boer journalist, 'for, notwithstanding the comparative clearness of the night, the difficulty of the ascent, and the earliness of the hour . . . the English surprised the piquet.'[1]

The darkness was still profound at 3.30 in the morning when Thorneycroft noted that the slope he was climbing was beginning to flatten out. One of his men whispered urgently that he could hear voices in the darkness ahead, and Thorneycroft quietly passed the word back to fix bayonets. The tension snapped when a party of engineers stumbled and dropped their picks and shovels, and a guttural 'Wies daar?' broke through the black silence. Acting on orders, the leading British files fell flat on their faces as the Boers emptied their magazines in their general direction. The moment the firing ceased Thorneycroft leapt to his feet and called for a charge which went in to cries of 'Majuba' and 'Bronkhorst Spruit'. It took his soldiers right over the enemy trenches. One burgher was bayoneted while the remainder fled precipately down the northern slopes, some still in their stockinged feet. The surprise had been complete. At the cost of three men wounded the British were masters of Spion Kop. As a member of the T.M.I. puts it 'the general

66

opinion amongst the men on the hill was that a bloodless victory had been gained'.[1]

Their charge had carried the soldiers on to the raised central dome of the plateau, and here they paused to regain their breath. Woodgate called for three cheers, the agreed signal, to inform Warren below that the summit had been secured, and at once the British artillery opened with a crash on the rear slopes of Spion Kop to harass any reinforcements that might be coming up for a counter-attack. Woodgate, who had no intention of repeating General Colley's mistake at Majuba Hill, now called on the engineers to lay out a trench system along the summit on the line where his men had halted. Meticulous officers laid down guide tapes, and the sappers began hacking at the hard earth with their picks and shovels. Unfortunately Woodgate did not bother to explore the ground slanting down gently in front of him. He assumed that the slope continued for some distance just as it had done on the rounded plateau of Thabanyama, and on the spur he had just ascended. He had no conception that a mere two hundred yards in front there was a crest line from which the ground fell away almost precipitously to the Ladysmith plain.

The soldiers did what they could to help the engineers but they were equipped with only light entrenching tools, and anyway were tired after their seven-hour march. Even so the engineers and their assistants dug away for three solid hours; everyone's attention was directed to the task and no attempt at all was made to investigate the ground in front. Dawn broke, at five, but a thick mist had settled on the summit of Spion Kop and the visibility, as one officer remarked, 'remained nil'.

For all their work on it the trench was disappointing. A Boer wrote, 'considering the number of men who could have taken part in the construction of the cover and to judge by the look of the meagre fortifications, the work had been unduly hurried over'. There was very little topsoil and the soldiers soon struck solid rock; at the end of three hours they had only raised a flimsy little wall of stones and rubbish some eighteen inches high in front of a shallow scooped-out ditch. The low wall was irregular and only gave cover to a man lying prone. The ground was particularly hard on the right flank and there the soldiers pulled rocks round likely clumps of boulders to make rough sangars. A few yards to the rear of the main entrenchment a second support trench was begun, but it was even more inadequate; as an observer remarked, 'the infantry had worn themselves out on the hard and rocky ground' and now they preferred resting to digging.

The trench they had made extended for a little over 400 yards. There is some dispute about the exact length of this trench: some accounts state that it was no more than 200 yards long. It was centred on the dome-shaped summit of the plateau and was shaped like a boomerang or flattened V with its apex pointing northwards. The section on the left measuring 200 yards faced north-west and ended at a prominent group of boulders; it was manned by the Royal Lancasters while the two companies of the South Lancashires scooped out cover behind the boulders beyond. The T.M.I. and the Lancashire Fusiliers on their right shared the central 180-yards-long portion of the trench which faced due north. On the right the Fusiliers' section of the trench angled back sharply for a further 50 yards; it was then extended to the south by a few somewhat inadequate sangars echeloned one behind the other and extending almost as far as the steep slopes leading down to the hill's precipitous southern face.

At 7 a.m. the mist momentarily lifted. Peering through the foggy light the soldiers for the first time realised that their trench was badly sited. In front the field of fire extended for only 200 yards to the plateau's crest line. Conditions were even worse on the extreme right where the trench was a mere 80 yards from the crest. The mist was thick enough, however, to conceal the saddle which joins the two halves of Spion Kop together, and the soldiers were still unaware that 400 yards away it humped up into Aloe Knoll, high enough to command and enfilade their position.

Military errors are cumulative: the sandbags had been forgotten, the mountain battery had not arrived, and now between

68

3.30 a.m. and 7 a.m. not one of Woodgate's 1,700 soldiers had been sent out to explore the forward summit of Spion Kop. There had seemed little point in doing anything but catch up on their broken sleep, because as one drowsy officer explained: 'A dense white cloud . . . enveloped the mountain top and blotted out vision beyond a distance of fifty yards at the most.'[1] But the great advantage they had gained was to vanish with the morning mist; the British soldiers unknowingly had dug their own graves when they entrenched in the centre of the plateau and had ignored the well established military principle that on a table-topped hill there are only two places to hold—either the forward crest, or a position immediately behind the rear crest. As it was, their entrenchment could have hardly been more dangerously situated: a large part of it was even aligned on the commanding position of Aloe Knoll which the Boers had already occupied. It was no wonder, a burgher later remarked, that the Tommies had got themselves into a 'noodlothige posisie'[2]—a fatal position.

In war, battles are not lost merely by making mistakes; they also require an alert enemy to take advantage of them. During the early hours of the 24th January the Boers' sure instinct for survival had made them take this advantage, and they had done it with the smoothness that is the essence of the art of war. Moving unseen through the mist they had managed to secure several points which commanded the British position. Within three hours they had turned apparent disaster into the beginnings of victory. The credit for this startling outcome belongs for the most part to Acting-Commandant-General Louis Botha, but much of it must be given to two of his subordinate officers, Commandants Opperman and Prinsloo, whose Pretoria and Carolina commandos had been laagered behind Green Hill and Twin Peaks respectively.

Botha had been awakened in his headquarters on a hillock a little north of Spion Kop by the sound of rifle fire. This was followed by cheering from the summit, and he knew at once that the British had surprised him and punched a hole into his defence line. Minutes later fugitives of the Vryheid commando carried a collection of vivid scare stories into the Boer laagers. Everyone jumped to the conclusion that seizure of Spion Kop was but part of an overwhelming general offensive, and nearly all the burghers hastily packed up their wagons and began to take off in them across the Ladysmith plain.

Nearly all of them, but not Louis Botha. There is an air of inspired desperation about the way he proceeded to deal with the crisis. He resolved to recapture the hill at all costs. He ran on to the Rosalie road with his secretary Jonkheer G. C. S. Sandberg and called on the fugitives to halt; one burgher saw Botha actually hitting some Boers who were disinclined to enter the fight, and heard him shouting 'Look at those foreigners; they have no home to defend, no liberty to lose, and they fight. Go and do the same.'[1] He sent horsemen galloping down the line as far as Acton Homes, Vaal Krantz and the Boer laagers round Ladysmith, all with messages calling up reinforcements to the threatened sector. He ordered three of his 'messengers'—Wolfaardt, Moll, and Slegtkamp (who had distinguished himself on Thabanyama three days before)—to ascend Aloe Knoll with Commandant Opperman and spy out the enemy position; this they did and went one better when they crept from Aloe Knoll through the mist on to the crest of Spion Kop itself where they found 'British soldiers everywhere'.[2] Botha also ordered all available guns into positions where they could shell the summit of the Kop. Before dawn he had mustered 400 burghers at the foot of the hill, and had set them moving up to assault the plateau. It was a prodigious effort and it was all accomplished with incredible speed and efficiency.

Commandant Hendrik Prinsloo reacted to the loss of Spion Kop with an energy fully equal to that of Louis Botha; indeed some Transvaalers still maintain that he is the real hero of the battle which followed. Prinsloo was a man of thirty-eight who had fought against the British in 1881 and had seen service in several campaigns against recalcitrant Transvaal native chiefs. Shortly before the outbreak of the 1899 war he had been appointed Commandant of the Carolina burghers. Carolina is a small town in the eastern Transvaal, but in 1899 its commando was something of a *corps d'élite* in the Boer army: its men affected rather grandiose peace-time uniforms which owed something to St. Cyr and West Point, and its officers even wore swords on parade. The commando had been well trained by a German regular. It was unusual too in having a doctor on its strength, while a school teacher named Louis Bothma was particularly expert as a heliograph signaller.[1]

On the night of 23rd January, the Carolina commando had slept immediately under Spion Kop and had taken the precaution of keeping their horses saddled and ready for a move at short notice. They were awakened by the noise and cheers above them. Prinsloo immediately sent thirty of his men under Corporal Abraham Smit and ten men under Jan Grobler to investigate the situation on the summit while he rode over to Botha's tent to discuss the situation with him.[2]

While Grobler's men were ascending the north-western part of the Kop, Smit's burghers crept up the north-east slope to the summit and lay listening to the sounds of picks and shovels as the soldiers dug their trench. Two hours later Prinsloo, who had left his horses in the ravine between Aloe Knoll and Spion Kop, joined them with the remainder of the Carolina commando; with him too were some burghers from Heidelberg under Field-Cornet Steenkamp, as well as a few recently arrived men from Boksburg and Germiston. Prinsloo had orders from Botha to clear the British from the plateau, and these orders he now had to communicate to his men. Even after all these years one can still see the scene in the imagination: the massive bearded figure of Prinsloo whispering to the burghers on the foggy crest line and the quiet withdrawal down the hill until it was judged that they were out of earshot of the soldiers, and then the urgent address to them: 'Burghers and friends,' he said, 'the choice of General Botha has fallen on us today to do a dangerous thing—we must all at costs drive the English from the positions they have taken from the Vryheiders. This I must also tell you; your lives are on a thread. It can be that not one of us will return.'[3] Then Prinsloo went on to say that those of the commando who wished to go back to the laager could do so without any reflection on their courage. Not a man moved. The entire commando instead climbed up the slope behind him again, lined the crest and extended themselves to the left on to Aloe Knoll, their movements still concealed from the British by the mist.[1]

There they were soon joined by Sarel Marais with fifty additional men from Heidelberg whom Botha had sent scrambling up to the saddle connecting Aloe Knoll to Twin Peaks. About the same time Field-Cornet Sarel Albert's commando from Germiston occupied Conical Hill while a strong force of Pretorians under Commandant Opperman dismounted and climbed up the north-western slopes of Spion Kop itself. Deneys Reitz, who had galloped with the Pretoria commando to the sound of guns, tells us how impressed he was by the 'hundreds of saddled horses in long rows'[2] standing patiently below the Kop where their owners left them. Another group of burghers from Heidelberg and Utrecht were meanwhile quietly taking up positions on Green Hill where they would enfilade the British left flank, and it fell to these men to open the Boer counter-attack with long-range rifle fire.

Rather than attempt the storming of Spion Kop, Botha's first concern was to use the milky obscurity of the morning to secure strong-points commanding Woodgate's position. By 7 a.m. he had succeeded. The right wing of the Carolina burghers was hidden behind the Kop's crest less than two hundred yards from the unsuspecting British soldiers. Aloe Knoll and Green Hill were both strongly held and, most important of all, Botha had been well briefed on the situation; as soon as the sun broke fleetingly through the mist the signaller, Louis Bothma, had got his heliograph into action on the slope below Aloe Knoll. It was with great relief that Botha learned that the British had not got a cannon on to the summit of the Kop.

At 7.30 a.m. the mist lightened again and the soldiers learned with dramatic suddenness that the Boers intended to dispute their possession of Spion Kop. A murderous fire swept the summit. The British were taken completely by surprise: one burgher tells us that they were 'enjoying the luxuries of an early picnic' at the moment of confrontation; their first casualty is said to have been a subaltern who was shot as he raised a sandwich of 'gentleman's relish' to his lips. A German observer with the Boers has this to say about the beginning of the fighting: 'When it was light it was found that we had formed a thin skirmishing line, in which there were hardly more than 200 or 250 rifles on the north-western, northern and north-eastern edges. We suddenly saw the British standing and kneeling in swarms about 300 yards to our front. They fired some volleys and then charged with the bayonet, but when about 100 or 150 yards from us they were thrown back, and several groups of them tried to rush separate points in our line, without, however, gaining any success'.[1]

On the whole the British recovered from the first shock of surprise very well. Their officers led spirited rushes to the crest line and after some hard hand-to-hand fighting they succeeded in dislodging the Boers from it. This was a solid achievement and if they had been given the time they could have still remedied the bad siting of their trench by digging another one on the crest line. But time was not granted them; the ground at the crest in any case was even harder than at the plateau's centre, and the engineers had taken off their heavy picks and spades to make a road up the hill for the expected guns to come up. The only cover for the soldiers was that provided by the boulders fringing the crest.

Still, the situation seemed to have been restored; the Boers had been evicted from the vital crest line and Woodgate felt confident enough to settle down at his command post for a cup of tea. He was admittedly a little concerned because his signal station had failed to establish communications with Task Force Headquarters, and at 7.45 Woodgate despatched à Court down the hill with a written report for Warren: 'we have entrenched a position', it said, 'and are I hope secure', but Woodgate added, 'fog is too thick to see'.[2] The message went on to suggest that twelve-pounder guns be hauled up to the summit in place of the missing mountain battery, and also that Lyttelton's brigade might ease pressure on his front by making a demonstration against Twin Peaks. à Court too was in an optimistic mood when he began the descent, and we must remember that the mist had not yet allowed him to make out the ominous slopes of Aloe Knoll. The British position, he assured a friend, 'could be held till doomsday against all comers'. At the bottom of the hill he borrowed a horse and at 9 a.m., after the quickest descent of Spion Kop made by any Britisher that day, he was at Three Tree Hill giving Warren his account of the situation.

Warren relaxed. Everything seemed to be going well. He had no idea that during à Court's hurried walk down the hill the situation had disastrously changed and that at 8.15 a.m. the acting British Commander on the summit of Spion Kop had sent a despairing signal to him which read 'reinforce at once or all lost. General dead.'[1] When it finally reached Three Tree Hill after being relayed from Spearman's, the message hit General Warren like the slam of a bullet.

6

BATTLE

There has never been another fight quite like Spion Kop. Men have died in greater numbers during scores of other battles both before and afterwards, but never was their dying concentrated into so small an area. Nor was there ever such a spotlighted gladiatorial character to a battle as there was to the montage of horror on Spion Kop. For after general action had been joined, the struggle on its summit was watched until darkness by thousands of onlookers. It was fought as though on the elevated stage of a gigantic theatre, and in full sight of most of the soldiers in Buller's army. The memory of their powerlessness to intervene remained with them all their lives. Churchill, who began the day on Spearman's Hill, has recorded that 'it drove us all mad to watch idly in camp' while the battle was going on; he compared the scene and the fighting men to 'a shadow peepshow' and wrote that 'along the mighty profile of the hill a fringe of little black crotchets advanced. Then there were brown and red smudges of dust from shells. Shells striking the ground and white puffs from shrapnel bursting in the air.'[1]

Buller had a particularly good view of the fighting from Mount Alice, and someone nearby was reminded by him of Xerxes sitting on his hill above the Hellespont. Through his telescope the General was even able to recognise individuals whom he knew on Spion Kop. Botha from his own camp on the smaller elevation near the Rosalie road could see the fighting less clearly, but thanks to the signalling expertise of his commandants he had a very precise conception of the ebb and flow of the battle. Warren, who of all people should have made sure he was in the best position to watch and control the fighting, was in fact in the worst. His camp faced on to the south-western spur of Spion Kop two miles away; he was too short-sighted (despite his monocle) for the summit to be more than a blur, while neither Aloe Knoll nor Twin Peaks beyond were visible from Three Tree Hill. From a tactical point of view he was too far away from Spion Kop to be able to direct the battle personally, yet too close to form a proper conception of its course, especially as the signalling arrangements between the summit and his headquarters were deplorable. One of the heliographs rigged up on the plateau was smashed by a bullet soon after the fighting began, and the other was too exposed to be used; flag signals from the firing lines were almost impossible to read on Three Tree Hill. Warren in consequence had to rely for information on messengers who took anything up to three hours to reach him. There was, to be sure, nothing to prevent Warren from moving his headquarters forward a mile or two and so cutting down the time lapse, but this never seems to have occurred to him.

There were many other spectators of the battle. More than thirty thousand people in and around Ladysmith—the garrison, the civilian population, and the Boers investing the place—had long-range views of the fight. 'Far away in the distance,' a doctor in the town wrote, 'we could see little white balls of smoke breaking over the summit', and he could hear 'the incessant roar of musketry all day'.[1] It was a hot and windy morning and other accounts from Ladysmith speak of the clouds of red dust and yellow lyddite smoke which swirled continuously across the summit of the Kop; but sometimes through their glasses White's officers could distinguish tiny figures scrambling about the battlefield and occasionally stopping to dig entrenchments. Then, too, thousands of Africans in the area came out of their kraals and all day long watched the madness of the white men being enacted in a narrow confine at the top of the highest hill for miles around.

If Spion Kop had something of the quality of a theatrical production for its distant onlookers, to those involved in the fighting the world had contracted into the narrow segment of rocky soil which they could cover with their rifles, and everything else dissolved into a haze of noise, wounds and death. Very few men on the summit had much idea of what was happening less than fifty yards away from where they were fighting.

Theirs became a hell set apart and separate from the rest of humanity, for while all was horror on the summit, all remained peace on the plain below.

The full appreciation of their peril burst upon the British when the sun finally burned the mist away at about 8.30 a.m. The soldiers on the crest line, and those in the shallow trench behind were immediately swept by continuous rifle fire. The shooting came in chiefly from the flanks—from Green Hill and Aloe Knoll and Conical Hill. The wide arc of fire covered every inch of the summit. Under its cover the Boers were able to scramble up Spion Kop's northern slopes again and regain the crest line. More fierce hand-to-hand fighting then broke out—the fighting of men jabbing forward with bayonets at men taking snap shots and swinging rifle butts above their heads. There were to be many other episodes of close-in fighting during the Boer War but the clash on that Wednesday morning was something different: each mêlée here was a fight to the finish, everybody who died died hard, nobody broke and nobody ran away. German observers were amazed that the initial struggles along the crest line did not end with one side or the other retreating; they only ended when the men on one side or the other were dead. Both Woodgate and the Boer commandants fed reinforcements into this hand-to-hand fighting which would swing in a wild line from the crest to the trench and back again. Sometimes it would die away when the British got a firm hold on the crest, and then the soldiers' ordeal became even worse as they crouched behind its necklace of boulders or pressed their faces against the stony soil, for the din of close combat fighting would now be replaced by the terrible clamour of rifle fire from Aloe Knoll until the soldiers were nearly all dead or the survivors had fallen back again to the doubtful shelter of the main trench.

We can see now that this struggle for the crest line marks the first of the four stages which can be discerned in the battle of Spion Kop. (The second stage was the Boer siege of the

77

main British trench and their attempt to storm it; the third phase was the drawn struggle for possession of the slopes of the hill to the right of the main trench; and the last stage was Botha's effort to destroy the soldiers on the summit with intensive shell fire.)

While the fighting for the crest line was still going on Colonel Bloomfield at the western end of the main trench was shaken to see large numbers of burghers streaming up Spion Kop's north-western slopes to join the fight. He called Woodgate over: as the two men stood there watching, a burst of shrapnel mortally wounded Woodgate above the right eye. He was supported to an advanced dressing station which had been set up 'where the mimosa blossomed' on the uppermost platform of the south-west spur. The troops were shaken to see him carried away and moaning, 'Let me alone, let me alone'.[1] Bloomfield took over the command on the summit but he too was wounded soon afterwards and the command passed to the next senior officer, Colonel Crofton.

No one seems to have been very impressed by Crofton's performance at Spion Kop, and certainly his first action as Commander was that of a man overwrought by his sudden responsibility: he decided to send an urgent message for help to Warren. No thought had been given to running a telephone line from Warren's headquarters up to the summit of Spion Kop although the equipment was available, and now the heliograph operator could not be found. A crawling search, however, discovered a Private Goodyear who said he could signal semaphore. Crofton told him to transmit: 'General Woodgate dead. Reinforcements urgently required.'[2] Goodyear in his excitement thought it would be as well to improve on Crofton's wording and the flag signal he finally got off read: 'Reinforce at once or all lost. General dead.' A few moments later Private Goodyear was blown to pieces, but his panicky message made an important contribution to the tragedy of Spion Kop. For although the British troops were in a serious position it was by no means as desperate as the message suggested. Admittedly it looked as though all but the western extremity of the crest would have to be abandoned to the Boers and the soldiers were being subjected to heavy shelling, as well as to rifle fire, but the main trench was firmly held and the Boers were sustaining heavy casualties too.

These should have been still heavier if the British artillery had been anything like as enterprising as the enemy's: as it was, their only success occurred when a burst of shell-fire succeeded in driving the burghers off Conical Hill.

The British guns, although ten times more numerous than the Boers', were badly handled; according to Botha they frequently shelled their own troops. On only one other occasion did the field guns seriously hurt the Boers when they opened a heavy fire on Aloe Knoll. By an unlucky chance Warren noticed their shells bursting on a position which all through the fight he assumed to be held by his men; so now he sent off an indignant message to the artillery commander which read: 'We occupy the whole summit and I fear you are shelling us seriously; cannot you turn your guns on the enemy guns.'[1] The batteries shifted at once to other targets, and the Boers continued in possession of Aloe Knoll almost unscathed. Perhaps the most absurd facet of this incident is that Buller from his vantage point could see that in fact Aloe Knoll was held by the Boers, but he failed to overrule Warren's request: it was said that he was too 'courteous' to interfere in his subordinate's tactical handling of the battle. Sometimes it seems that he almost wanted Warren to lose it.

The Boer guns were few but they were brilliantly served, and after 9 a.m. it was their shells as much as rifle fire which harassed the soldiers. Botha had skilfully sited his guns behind hills which hid them from Warren's batteries; with one exception they all fired smokeless powder and they were never spotted, let alone silenced, by counterfire. Two 6-inch Creusot 'Long Toms' were placed on the rear slope of Green Hill only 4,200 yards from the summit of Spion Kop. He hid a Krupp and a pompom even closer to the western edge of the battle. The Krupp which had been hauled half way up Spion Kop when Warren seized the summit was hastily pulled back to

Botha's headquarters where a pompom had already been set up. A third Krupp was concealed on the slope behind Twin Peaks some 2,800 yards from the summit, while a pompom was pushed still further forward on this flank. All these guns commanded the crowded hilltop from an arc of 120°. Theirs was the sort of target gunners dream of, and the guns were so well handled that they consistently dropped their shells on to British soldiers only fifty yards away from the Boer positions. Thorneycroft reported later that the enemy bombardment 'was very accurate, the bursting of the shells was well timed and swept the whole length of the plateau'.[1] Churchill watching from below counted seven shells bursting on the summit every minute,[2] and someone standing by the Tugela noticed that the shock of their percussion 'made even the bosom of the placid silvery river shudder and quake'.[3]

Just as the British artillery was far less effective than that of the enemy, so in comparison was the soldiers' rifle fire. They had been taught to fire on command in volleys rather than to shoot at individual targets as the present situation demanded. Moreover, training programmes issued from the Horse Guards had not encouraged, but rather had positively frowned upon, exhibitions of tactical initiative. And now the soldiers were exposed to some of the most accurate marksmen in the world firing at them from concealed positions at short range. The troops were particularly vulnerable to the fire coming from Aloe Knoll on their right flank: after the battle seventy men of the Lancashire Fusiliers were found dead in the trench with bullet holes in the right side of their heads. Compared with their exposure, the burghers had splendid cover on the rough ground of Aloe Knoll or behind the fringe of boulders which ran along the northern crest line of the plateau proper. There they were able to keep watch with a few men, while their comrades rested in comparative safety some yards down the slope: but when the cry of 'the Khakis are coming' went up, every man scrambled back and most of the charges which the soldiers put in died away short of the crest.

The soldiers found that they obtained better results when

they approached the enemy more stealthily, moving forward from rock to rock; sometimes in this way they succeeded in reaching the crest line without much loss and touched off new flurries of hand-to-hand fighting. An idea of the conditions during these clashes comes from the report that when a certain Private Bradford of the Lancastrians cautiously raised his rifle over a rock in front of him, 'it struck something soft: in his excitement he pulled the trigger: the soft substance was the waistcoat of a Boer . . .'[1] A startled war correspondent watching one of these movements from below wrote that 'the trench was notched against the sky like a saw—made I supposed of sharp rocks built into a rampart. Another shell struck it, and then— heavens!—the trench rose up and moved forward. The trench was men; the teeth against the sky were men. They ran forward bending their bodies into a curve.'[2]

The Boer line once gave way in front of Aloe Knoll but as always there was an officer among them who rose to the crisis: Commandant Prinsloo saw men from the Carolina commando slipping away from their positions pursued by soldiers with fixed bayonets. He shouted to them to take cover behind a convenient ledge on the slope: then he rallied them, shot all the unwary soldiers and got his men back to crest line. The Boers considered this counter-attack to be one of the climactic episodes of the action: 'This is where the battle of Spion Kop was won,' writes one of their memorialists.[3]

The ebb and flow of battle persisted all through the first half of that hot morning with the disputed crest line the prize for both sides, and it reminded one watching journalist of 'a perilous game of seesaw'.[4] The soldiers spent most of their time crouching in their trench or lying on their bellies in the dusty grass behind a life-saving rock, the heat of the sun crushing their backs, bullets whip-lashing over them, and shells bursting like the crack of doom above, while Prinsloo's voice thirty yards away could be heard shouting 'shoot fast, men, shoot and shoot to kill'.[5] But three or four times in every hour the soldiers would respond to their officers' calls for another counter-attack into the smoking fog on the summit; the gun smoke now would be lit by sparkling spurts of fire, and they endured yet another few minutes of concentrated fury of bullets.

By 11 a.m. the Boers' hold on the crest had become firm except at its extreme western sector where a handful of the T.M.I. maintained their position during the remainder of the day. Their salient, one trooper explained, 'was protected by a fold in the ground which runs rectangularly from the crest line towards the entrenchment',[1] and this gave them some protection from enfilading fire.

A German officer has left us an account of the end of the fighting for the crest: 'After their onslaughts had come to grief,' he writes, 'the British rushed back and formed a firing line which stretched in a gentle curve right across the plateau at about its centre. A steady fire fight opened. At first both sides shot so wildly that one's senses were almost paralysed by the quite too awful din.'[2]

Now the only results from the British charges were the deaths of a few more men and the further inextricable mixing of the weary survivors from different units. The soldiers had lost all sense of time by now, the fighting seemed to have become unplanned and formless. But still they went on trying to regain the crest: 'time and time again with their brave officers ahead,' one admiring burgher tells us, 'the British troops attacked us, but time and time again they were mowed down.'[3]

Individual acts of heroism and cowardice of soldiers and burghers alike were all swallowed up in the monstrous confusion of this struggle. But after each spasm of fighting had ebbed away the soldiers' lives became incredibly circumscribed again: what went on twenty yards away seemed to have become of no significance; each man was isolated in the small area of his immediate experience; few of them had any thought in their heads except an obsessive wish to slake their savage thirsts and a modest aspiration to keep alive through the hours that were left to nightfall. And yet they clung to the main trench: the plateau for them had become more than a disputed piece of ground; it had also become a cause to die for.

Until they received Crofton's agitated message, 'reinforce at once or all lost. General dead', both Buller and Warren had passed comparatively uneventful mornings. Instead of riding over to consult with Warren as had been his custom during the last few days, Buller had plodded up instead to the signal station above his tent and watched the fighting through his glass. It was very peaceful up there. Doves were cooing among the trees, and nursing sisters from the nearby hospital walked about in their shade and, as one officer pointed out, 'relieved our eyes of the continual sight of nothing but khaki'.[1] The battle was too far away for any of its horrors really to impinge on a man's senses at Spearman's camp. Buller felt happy too in the thought that if anything was going wrong it could not be blamed on him. He cocooned himself in a sense of irresponsibility and stared at the deadliest fighting in South African history with an almost clinical detachment. If the operation went well he would, no doubt, be able to claim most of the credit; if it failed the fault would clearly be Warren's. It was almost an irritation when odd signals from the fighting line came into Spearman's, but they were enough to invite him to interfere from time to time in the course of the battle: he would send a kindly suggestion to Warren or polite messages of warning. One officer watching him that morning put it very well when he said that the General had 'commented rather than commanded'[2] at Spion Kop, and another man's remark was hardly less apt when he noted that Sir Redvers' messages were 'the voice of a spectator or critic expressing a somewhat agitated concern and offering a piece of advice'.[3] The trouble was that Warren not unnaturally regarded the recommendations he received from Spearman's as orders, and acted on them all. Buller further sometimes so far forgot his self-imposed role of impartial umpire as to send positive instruction to subordinate commanders who were near at hand. Every time he did so these direct orders were followed by disastrous results.

Warren had been scarcely more active than the placid Buller that Wednesday morning. At 7 a.m. he had roused himself to ride over to the base of Spion Kop; he stayed there for an hour or so but there seemed little for him to do there, and presently he was back at his more agreeable headquarters two miles away.

But at 10 a.m. he was startled and stung into a rush of activity by Crofton's despairing message. He had already despatched two supporting battalions—the Imperial Light Infantry and Middlesex Regiment—up Spion Kop; now he responded to the crisis by telling General Coke to climb the hill with the Dorset Regiment and to assume command on the summit; his final words to him were 'mind, no surrender'.[1] Then Sir Charles addressed himself to the technicalities of getting water, food, and ammunition up to the soldiers on Spion Kop. He found time for a nap, however, and he made no attempt to relieve pressure on the summit by employing the additional 10,000 men he had available on a subsidiary attack— although in a moment of distress it appears that he did appeal to Lyttelton for help. What still strikes us as strange is that Warren displayed no wish to see what was going on on the top of Spion Kop for himself; perhaps he was convinced that a battle of this sort was best controlled from a command post well away from the firing line, but even so there was nothing to prevent him from advancing his headquarters to the base of the hill.

Warren had always wanted General Coke to fight the battle of Spion Kop; now by sending him up the hill he had got his way, for Coke would be the ranking officer on the summit. Unhappily Coke was no hustler. His lameness from a scarcely healed fracture of the leg may have explained his slowness in climbing, but it hardly accounted for the three vital hours Coke spent on the mimosa plateau 600 feet below the summit; one suspects that the unkind reports that he dropped off to sleep there may have been true. The schedule of his movements is clear enough: General Coke began the ascent of Spion Kop some time before 11 a.m.; he reached the mimosa ledge on its shoulder an hour afterwards; he appeared below the southern edge of the plateau (though not on the summit proper) at 5.30 that afternoon and returned thankfully to his ledge about an hour later. His small exertions all now seem very pointless, but Coke did have one good idea when he went up Spion Kop and it might have won the battle for him: he took a machine-gun along when he began the climb—but, as he was to explain later, 'unfortunately it overturned'.[1]

Meanwhile, conditions on the summit were making less and less sense to the troops in the main trench. They are subjected to continuous rifle and shell fire by an invisible enemy and events seemed to have been overtaken by futility: messages are for ever being sent off to Warren, but none of them ever arrive; officers stand up to shout to each other but no one can hear a word of what they say through the prodigious din; Indian water-carriers stand in tears far away at the bottom of the hill because the biscuit tins which are to be used to carry water to the desperately thirsty troops have not been sent over the Tugela; wounded soldiers on the summit are hit again or broken apart by shells and rock splinters; to peer over their little runs of earth for the soldiers is to court instant death; to creep to the rear for water or to have a wound dressed or to fulfil a call of nature risks a bullet from an enemy sharpshooter only seventy yards away. The mistakes and misunderstandings continue to go on hour after hour. There is no direction to this battle, just a grim hanging on to a broken-down trench. Clearly there was something desperately wrong here. Errors and muddles have occurred in plenty, yet still one has the feeling that none of them are bad enough to have made things go quite so badly as they have gone. Of course the bungling and dismal lack of leadership given to the soldiers by 'Bulldog' Buller and 'Jerusalem' Warren can account for much of the trouble, and a good deal can be blamed too on the faulty tactical lessons the British officers had learned in the Long Valley at Aldershot and then applied here on Spion Kop, but between them all these factors simply do not add up enough to account for all that has gone amiss, and one is left with the feeling that there still remains some mysterious element in this battle which so far has been unrecognised.

We hear little of Crofton during the fighting for the main trench, but all reports agree that Thorneycroft was the heart and kernel of the British defence. This was a soldier's fight; especially it was Thorneycroft's fight and he waged it in a frenzy, filling the soldiers with his aggressive spirit and propping up their courage with his own. The descriptions of his bravery are numerous. He roars from one threatened sector to another; time after time he leads another knot of men to regain a patch of lost ground, until at 11 o'clock that morning he falls heavily in a mêlée and twists his knee badly. And all the time the odds are favouring the Boers: the second phase of the battle has begun for the main British trench is now under siege and repeated assault. 'In places,' writes one burgher observer, 'the Mausers had actually torn and raked away the parapet of the trenches through sheer press of bullets';[1] reinforcements are reaching the Boers proportionately faster than they are the British, and so is ammunition which is being carried up to them in jute bags by coloured servants. Two hundred fresh men come up in a single mass with Tobias Smuts from beyond Twin Peaks after he has telegraphed to Joubert that 'the fighting with General Botha is very fierce. Because his positions are very important I am going there myself with part of the Standerton people. As a result of this I am exposing my positions here. This cannot be avoided. Help must be given. If the positions held by General Botha are lost we have lost everything. All must be sacrificed for these positions.' By now the Boer fighting commandants had decided among themselves that Opperman should command the centre of the battle while Prinsloo assumed responsibility for what went on on the vital eastern flank. The threat from Aloe Knoll increased as his men of the Carolina commando began to advance on to the right extremity of the British trench and infiltrated under cover of the hill's south-eastern slopes around its rear. There was little now to stop them: the trench itself was choked with dead and wounded; the survivors were exhausted and parched with thirst, and most of them had had no food all day; they seemed to be breathing not air now but gun smoke and the stench of death; their ammunition was in short supply and although a small amount of muddy water was available at a spring the

Green Hill

Conical Hill

Summit Spion Kop

Upper ledge

Middle ledge

S.W. Spur

Ravine between
Green Hill and
Spion, Kop

Precipitous N.W. face of Skop

Lowest
ledge

View of Spion Kop from Three Tree Hill

Spion Kop and Twin Peaks, north-eastern aspect

Aerial view of Spion Kop

(*see plan opposite*)

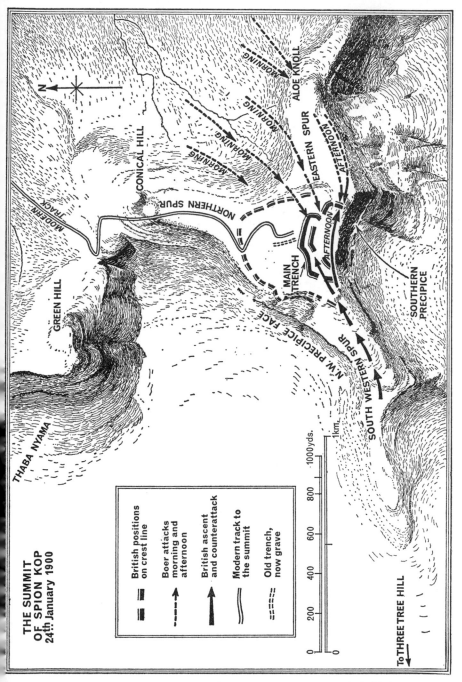

THE SUMMIT
OF SPION KOP
24th January 1900

British positions
on crest line

Boer attacks
morning and
afternoon

British ascent
and counterattack

Modern track to
the summit

Old trench,
now grave

THABA NYAMA

GREEN HILL

MODERN TRACK

CONICAL HILL

NORTHERN SPUR

N.W. PRECIPICE FACE

MAIN TRENCH

MORNING

MORNING

MORNING

MORNING

ALOE KNOLL

EASTERN SPUR

AFTERNOON

AFTERNOON

AFTERNOON

SOUTHERN PRECIPICE

SOUTH WESTERN SPUR

N

0   200   400   600   800   1000 yds.

km.

To THREE TREE HILL

G

engineers had opened on the summit, and more in a depot just below the southern crest, the soldiers might reach it only through the gauntlet of fire that separated them. They could but keep their heads down. Often now the only movement to be seen on the summit of Spion Kop was the dragging crawl of a wounded man towards a boulder which promised him better cover. But below the southern crest soldiers are milling about on the slope, too proud to desert, too scared to return to the summit, but frightened enough to rush in desperate little groups from the shelter of one fold of ground to another as the enemy guns shift to fresh targets. About midday the Boers began to gain more of the plateau, determined now to win a second Majuba. 'From most points,' one of them wrote, 'it was impossible to clearly see the British soldiers lying on the ground. So most of us began to push forward a foot or so at a time, the men next to one another firing and creeping by turns. In the course of an hour, we were able to creep forward 100 yards, some more, some less. At last the low earth heaps thrown up by the British could be seen almost without raising oneself. The two firing lines were now only separated by a level space on which lay but a few boulders; on to this the Boers did not advance.'[1]

Even after gaining the plateau proper the Boers still enjoyed better cover than the soldiers. As one burgher explained, 'taking it all round our irregular firing line was better sheltered than the British; besides which we could generally catch them obliquely as they were in a central position. The stupidity of the British soldiers also added to their disadvantages.'[2] But he adds, 'to me it is more than doubtful whether the burghers would have held out if the artillery had not hailed shrapnel and pompom shells over our heads into the enemy. The British rifle fire was constantly weakening, but when the firing line was reinforced it broke out again, to fade away once more. Sometimes the British sent forward from the rearmost sections could be seen as they advanced into the firing line; sometimes when they crawled along the ground they reached the front without being seen at all. Although many of them fell asleep the fire of the Boers never entirely ceased; they waited for the moment when a British helmet could be seen somewhere, to overwhelm it with fire from all sides so they soon ceased to appear. A few weak attempts to rush forward in a bayonet charge were crushed from the very outset.'[1]

The Boer commanders eventually got 600 men crouching behind the boulders in front of the trench; a heliograph message called on their artillery to cease firing as the burghers nerved themselves for the final charge which was to overwhelm the right flank of the British position. When it came their rush carried them clean up to the main trench; the Fusiliers by now had lost most of their officers and their will to fight was ebbing; handkerchiefs fluttered above the flimsy breastworks; soldiers got to their feet holding up hands in surrender and asking for water; at that moment it seemed that complete victory for the Boers was only ten minutes away. But there now occurred one of the most extraordinary events in an extraordinary battle: 'We should have had the whole hill,' laments Field-Cornet de Kock, 'the English were about to surrender when a great, big, angry-faced soldier ran out of a trench on our right and shouted "I am in command here. Take your men back to hell, sir. I allow no surrender." '[2]

There is a mixture of the ridiculous and the epic about the incident which de Kock describes. Thorneycroft, a little further down the trench, had seen the Fusiliers surrendering. He came up in limping, stumbling haste, overwhelmed the Boer commander with a torrent of shouted words while the burghers and soldiers stood around and looked on with gaping mouths; then, 'in order', as he says, 'not to get mixed up in any discussion',[3] he withdrew, taking along with him those soldiers who would listen to him, and before de Kock had a chance to protest he had got them under the cover of the southern crest. The right half of the trench was in Boer hands.

It was typical of the chaos at this time on the summit that a nearby English officer had only a foggy idea of what was happening: 'There was a great commotion a hundred yards or so on the right,' he says, 'men were standing up and gesticulating.

Surely those others with them could not be some of the enemy. The commotion died down and the firing went on as before.'[1] Another English observer catches the atmosphere of confusion when he wrote that 'there is panic on the right and all at once the cry is raised "The Lancs. are giving in". It is only too true. Nearly 200 had thrown down their arms and were marching down to the enemy. No one knew the reason and the question "Who's in command?" arose from several subordinate officers.'[2] Jan Celliers, a Boer Field-Cornet had a clearer view of this celebrated incident. He says that when the Fusiliers stood up in the trench, he led forward a party of Boers to accept their surrender, and it seemed to him that the story of Majuba Hill was about to be repeated. Over 180 soldiers were hustled down the hill as prisoners before Thorneycroft ran up, cowed the burghers with his shouting, and led the remaining men back to cover in a way which reminded yet another observer of a rugby team withdrawing down the field prior to taking a free kick.

At precisely that moment when Thorneycroft got his soldiers back to the crest, a company of the Middlesex Regiment came up from the rear. Thorneycroft shook them into a line with his own men and then led them all back in an irresistible bayonet charge which regained the trench. Moll and Wolfaardt, two of the burghers who had been the first to climb Aloe Knoll that morning, were killed in this fighting.[3]

Buller had seen it all. Only a few minutes earlier à Court, when reporting to him on Spearman's, had been full of praise for Thorneycroft's leadership during the ascent of Spion Kop, and now Sir Redvers had recognised his gigantic figure retrieving the situation just when the British troops were on the edge of disaster. Buller had been irritated by the wording of Crofton's despairing signal after Woodgate had been wounded and now it occurred to him that the mettlesome Thorneycroft would make a far better overall commander on the summit than the faint-hearted Crofton. And so Buller made a new contribution to the battle by telegraphing to Warren: 'Now Woodgate is dead, I think you must put a strong commander

90

on top: I recommend you put Thorneycroft in command.' (Buller's despatch of 30th January 1900 gives a slightly different version of this message: the relevant part reads, 'I could see that our men on the top of Spion Kop had given way and that efforts were being made to rally them. I telegraphed to Sir C. Warren: "Unless you put some really good hard fighting man in command on the top you will lose the hill. I suggest Thorney-croft."')[1] He repeated the same advice by runner: 'I think it [is] want of head in the CO than want of strength which makes the difficulty. They tell me that Crofton is not much good. I have telegraphed you to put Thorneycroft in command.'[2]

Warren could scarcely disobey General Buller's 'recommendation': he promptly heliographed Crofton that Thorneycroft was promoted to the local rank of Brigadier-General in command of the troops on the summit. One of his men has told us of the manner in which Thorneycroft learned of his promotion: 'Somebody said to him "Here's a messenger," and a man ran up with his lips shaped to speak. He was shot dead through the eye and fell across the Colonel's legs with his message undelivered. A few minutes after this Lieutenant Rose crept up behind a rock close at hand and shouted through the uproar "Sir C. Warren has heliographed to say that you are in command. You are a General." Rose added that the right was hard pressed, but he had seen reinforcements on their way up the hill.'[3] Unfortunately Warren forgot to inform General Coke, whom he had despatched up the hill scarcely an hour before to take charge on the summit, of the new command arrangements. The wretched Coke never heard of Thorneycroft's appointment until next day, and a tragi-comedy of utter confusion concerning the identity of the senior British officer on Spion Kop now began.

Only a little later Buller had another opportunity of interfering fatally in the course of the battle, and he did not fail to take it. Three fine battalions of Lyttelton's brigade were concentrated near Spearman's Camp that morning; they were doing nothing, and Lyttelton ached to get them into action when the shooting began on Spion Kop. At 10 a.m. he got his chance: he received a message from Warren asking for help and this was followed by an anxious helio signal from the summit which read: 'We occupy all the crest on top of the hill. Being heavily attacked from your side. Help us.'[1] Lyttelton decided later that this particular message came from an overwrought signaller and not from Warren, but at all events he decided that this was his chance to intervene in the battle; after talking things over with his Brigade Major, Henry Wilson, he ordered all three available battalions to 'Kaffir Drift', mid-way between Potgieter's and Trichardt's, and he had them across the river by 1 p.m.

His leading units, the Scottish Rifles under Colonel Cooke and Bethune's Mounted Infantry, were ordered to move directly on Spion Kop; after they had started off Lyttelton saw other reinforcements climbing the hill on the far side and he decided that his third battalion—the King's Royal Rifles—should march straight across the plain towards Twin Peaks.

Buller was furious at the way Lyttelton was interfering in Warren's battle and he thought the move he was making to be dangerous in the extreme. The King's Royal Rifles, he protested, would be annihilated; it was absurd, he said, to think that a single battalion would be able to drive the Boers from the heights when Warren's whole corps had failed to do so after five days' fighting. The loss of the Rifles, he grumbled too, would imperil the whole army and he sent an urgent message to Lyttelton ordering their recall. It was ignored with Nelsonian disobedience and, as Buller fumed, the K.R.R. opened out in skirmishing order and continued their advance.

Their attack was brilliantly conducted. While nearly everyone's attention remained concentrated on the struggle for the plateau of Spion Kop, the riflemen doggedly clambered up Twin Peaks. Resistance was minimal. At 5 o'clock that afternoon both peaks were in their possession and Schalk Burger's commando, which should have defended them, was in full flight towards Ladysmith.

This success had been something of a miracle. To the casual observer the southern slopes of Twin Peaks seem impossible for fully accoutred troops to scale, and one can only marvel at the prowess of these riflemen. Their success deserved and should have ensured a notable victory. The K.R.R. happened to have probed and broken the weakest part of the Boer position, and once they had secured the peaks there was nothing to prevent them turning westwards along the crestline and linking up with the soldiers on Spion Kop. Botha counted their advance as a far greater threat than the stalemate on the Kop's summit, and after sending off his staff officers to stiffen the wavering burghers, he threw in his only reinforcements— the twelve runners or messengers attached to his headquarters —to stop the rot. They failed: the panic of Schalk Burger's commandos quickly communicated itself to their neighbours and Prinsloo had some difficulty in preventing the indomitable Carolina men from abandoning Aloe Knoll. At the price of 20 men killed and 70 wounded the K.R.R. had punched another hole into the Boer position; now it seemed that nothing could prevent the British winning the battle.

But Buller still had to be reckoned with, and one can only wince away from the glaring folly he now proceeded to demonstrate. For he was determined to get the Rifles back, and for most of the afternoon he had pelted Lyttelton and Wilson with angry instructions to recall them. Henry Wilson knew Buller; he simply stuck the successive messages into his pocket, as though they did not exist (later on in the Natal campaign he was to push his insubordination a further notch when he tried to organise a revolt among the other Brigade Majors in the army, with the declared intent of arresting Sir Redvers and removing him from his command).[1] But his first attempt to thwart that dithering incompetent came to an end when Buller demanded to see copies of all the messages he had transmitted to Lyttelton's brigade; even Wilson could now no longer ignore him, and the Rifles were ordered to withdraw to their starting point. 'It was disgusting, heartbreaking, but it had to be done,' wrote one of their officers. As it was the battalion commander procrastinated as long as he could, and it was dark before the riflemen began to fall back to the river, but during the evening hours of opportunity after 5 p.m., Buller's peremptory order prevented them from exploiting a splendid opportunity of rolling up the Boer position.

We must note in parenthesis that the success of the K.R.R. on Twin Peaks can be ascribed in part to the very difficulty of the task they had been set: the slope the battalion ascended was so steep that for most of the way its men moved through dead ground. But they were also fortunate in facing a commando of poor quality; it was commanded by General Burger, a tall thin ascetic man with a black horse-shoe beard, who had earlier 'admitted he was not a soldier and unfit to command'; his men were infected by his spirit and refused to face the final bayonet charge which carried the crest. Far behind the line when Commandant-General Joubert learned that they were withdrawing he tried to rally the commando with assurances of support. 'I am sorry to see you wavering,' he signalled, 'trust in the Lord. Two hundred burghers from Rustenburg are on the way to help you. You must all work together and drive the enemy away again. Help one another with counsel and deed and united strength, and the Lord will add his blessing to that.' But Joubert's exhortations turned out to be unnecessary. Sir Redvers Buller was fighting on the British side.

The arrival of the first companies of the Middlesex Regiment on Spion Kop during the early afternoon of the battle had enabled Thorneycroft to restore the position in the main trench. The enemy effort reached its climax at about 1.30 p.m. but from then on the danger of the British being driven off the summit proper receded as more reinforcements were fed into the fight and the third stage of the battle began—Botha's attempt to outflank the trench along the hill's slopes.

Thorneycroft by now had been able to set up a proper battle headquarters where Woodgate had established himself that morning under the cover of a large group of boulders, and at 2.30 p.m. he wrote a situation report for Warren which ended: 'If you wish to really make a certainty of the hill for night you must send more infantry and attack enemy's guns.'[1] Coke intercepted this on its way down the hill and endorsed it with a confident, 'We appear to be holding our own', but he never seems to have enquired why Thorneycroft had written it as the officer commanding the summit.

Thorneycroft's attention was still riveted on the plateau and he was quite unaware that a separate battle by now had flared up a mere two hundred yards away on the south-eastern slopes of Spion Kop. For while the 2,000 men he commanded were busy keeping their heads down among the 500 dead and dying in what one officer described as 'this acre of massacre',[1] the Boers were attempting to envelop his command by pushing round its right flank below the southern lip of the plateau. More British reinforcements were now coming up the hill and they were directed to the right before reaching the lip. From there they moved east just above the southern precipice of the kop until they reached a place where the slope becomes more gradual and almost justifies being called a fourth, south-eastern, spur. It was here that the third phase of the battle of Spion Kop was fought out. It was pure chaos there on the hillside as fresh companies of the Middlesex Regiment, the I.L.I., Bethune's Mounted Infantry, and finally the Scottish Rifles were sucked into this separate struggle. Confused attacks and counter-attacks surged across the slopes in a wild reprise of the earlier fighting on the summit, and there were desperate struggles for positions which were no more than a few rocks or a shallow ledge in the ground.

Acting-Brigadier Thorneycroft and Colonel Hill commanding the Middlesex on the slopes below him both believed they were fighting the main battle and were so engrossed with it that they had no knowledge of the other's existence. For his part General Coke had no more than the vaguest idea of what was going on in either sector of the struggle.

On Three Tree Hill Warren continued to live in a sort of limbo of his own. Hardly any news was reaching him: the British signalling arrangements still remained almost completely disrupted, but a staff officer had persuaded Winston Churchill to climb the hill and try to discover what was going on. Warren's chief anxiety concerned the Mountain Battery which had still not turned up from Frere. He had intended sending it up the hill the moment it arrived and he was somewhat put out to receive a jocular note from Buller which told them: 'They will have a devil of a march. You must give them a rest before they go up.'[1]

At 4 p.m. Lieutenant Churchill arrived on the summit. He had already developed a talent for getting into interesting situations: during the past two months he had been captured by the Boers and had made a well-publicised escape from them. Now, newly commissioned in the South Africa Light Horse (but still doubling as a war correspondent), he had climbed up Spion Kop during the most critical period of the battle. On the slopes he encountered a disorderly coming and going of stragglers and broken sections seeking their units. 'Streams of wounded met us and obstructed the path,' he wrote later; 'men were staggering alone, or supported by comrades, or crawling on hands and knees or carried on stretchers. Corpses lay here and there. Many of the wounds were of a horrible nature. The splinters and fragments of the shells had torn and mutilated in the most ghastly manner. I passed about 200 while I was climbing up.' The chaos became worse as he approached the plateau. 'The scenes there,' he says, 'were among the strangest and most terrible I have ever witnessed', and he grimly noted that the feather in his slouch hat had been cut in two by a bullet. At this time the struggle for the south-eastern slopes was passing its crucial stage: repeated efforts by the Boers to get round the British flank had narrowly been beaten back by the timely arrival of reinforcements, and now the battle was going against them as the soldiers in their turn were counterattacking in an attempt to outflank Aloe Knoll.

The movement was unsuccessful but it made Botha give up all hope of driving the soldiers off the plateau; his burghers were no less exhausted now than the soldiers. 'We were hungry, thirsty and tired, and around us were the dead men covered with swarms of flies attracted by the smell of blood', Deneys Reitz tells us, and Botha was unable to call on them for any more direct assaults. But he did not admit defeat: he decided to contain the British troops and destroy them by continuous shell fire, and thus opened the final phase of the battle of Spion Kop. The burghers withdrew behind the hill's crest and the Boer artillery swept the summit of the Kop in a continuous drumfire. 'Everywhere,' wrote a British officer, 'was the same deadly smash of the shells, mangling and killing all about us.'[1]

At 5.30 Coke nerved himself to leave his sheltered shelf on the hillside and he climbed up to where the Middlesex Regiment was taking cover on the upper slopes of the hill. There he was surprised to find a 'scene of considerable confusion',[2] with units mixed up together and no one quite sure whose orders to follow since the officers had removed their badges of rank before going into action. Eventually Coke made contact with Colonel Hill; he did not attempt to reach the summit proper or to see Thorneycroft, but at this point we must remember, as Coke was later at pains to explain, that 'no word had reached me of Lieutenant-Colonel Thorneycroft's appointment to command and I regarded him simply as a junior brevet Lieutenant-Colonel in command of a small unit' who was 'assisting Colonel Crofton in a portion of the front line'.[3]

It was one of the strangest aspects of the battle of Spion Kop that four British acting General officers were at this moment on the hill and three of them at least believed themselves to be the supreme commander: Coke had good reason to; he was by far the most senior and he had been personally entrusted by Warren with the task of holding the position. One sympathises with the others too: Hill was acting Brigadier-General of the 10th Brigade and he knew nothing of Thorneycroft's sudden promotion, while Thorneycroft had been notified of his succession to the supreme command by a message from Warren and like Hill he had no idea that Coke had come three-quarters of the way up the hill to the uppermost ledge. Even Crofton was uncertain where he stood; his feelings, he said, had been 'hurt most deeply [at] being superseded during an engagement by an officer so much my junior',[4] but he was somewhat grudgingly prepared to accept Thorneycroft's new position. To add to the confusion Colonel Cooke of the newly arrived Scottish

Rifles demurred at taking orders from Thorneycroft, and he spent some time trying to work out the puzzle of command by getting Coke and Thorneycroft to meet each other and discuss it. He did not succeed and the confusion continued. Although perhaps its bad effects have been exaggerated in accounts of the battle, since each commander devoted his attention to different sectors of the battlefield, it was no wonder that Lord Dundonald wrote afterwards that 'the selection of Lt.-Colonel Thorneycroft to take command over his seniors in the heat of action was a singular example of the danger of a serious departure from precedent at such a time';[1] he went on to say that: 'It would take pages to describe the different forms of muddling that took place in connection with Spion Kop; one might as well attempt to describe what happens to various wheels in a clock when the mainspring is out of order.'[2]

Coke on the slope was at least able to see that Twin Peaks was in British hands. He was also in a position to order a determined attack which would pinch out Aloe Knoll and so secure the British position. But no thought of offensive action was in his mind that afternoon. Instead he solemnly charged Hill with holding the summit through the night and thankfully returned to the signal station on the upper shelf of the southwest spur from which he presently got off a message to Warren, tentatively suggesting withdrawal from Spion Kop.

And yet when the sun began to go down over the distant Drakensberg at 6 o'clock that evening, and the summit was dim with twilight and the piled-up battle smoke, thanks to the steadiness and endurance of the ordinary soldier and despite all the Generals' muddling, the British had virtually won the battle of Spion Kop. They had held the summit against direct assault and had beaten off the Boers' attempts to envelop them along the southern slopes. Twin Peaks was firmly in their hands and threatened the vital salient of Aloe Knoll. Immense numbers of reserves were available to reinforce or relieve the troops on the plateau. Food, water and ammunition were all coming up the hill. The mountain battery was approaching at this time and could soon begin the ascent, while slides for heavier naval guns and cables to haul them to the top were being prepared for their arrival. Warren had even belatedly sent for a balloon which he recollected having seen at Frere; when it arrived next day he would be able to grasp the tactical situation of his troops on the Kop and direct them accordingly. All that the soldiers had to do now was to hang on to their positions through the night, and Spion Kop would go down to history as a glorious British victory. It only needed a single spasm of initiative by General Warren, or even a short message of encouragement from him to give Colonel Thorneycroft and his men the resolution that was required. But neither came; the mistakes and blunders continued to occur as though they had attained an irresistible momentum of their own.

When the light began to fade nearly all the Boers had admitted defeat. The official history of the South African War records that 'by night fall every laager and most of the guns were on the move to the rear, the stormers of Spion Kop, utterly exhausted, slipped away one by one, four of the commandos from the actual front were riding from the passes, and there arose signs of a panic throughout the whole Federal forces.'

Botha himself was exhausted; when it grew dark he walked down from the command post to rest and to take some food in his tent. But still he would not admit defeat. Instinct told him that the British would throw away their victory. Although he kept falling asleep during its dictation, he composed a despatch for Joubert in which he advised him that 'the enemy had taken a well sheltered position in order to be able to leave after dark and thus avoid surrendering more prisoners'. If necessary, however, he was prepared to renew the fight next morning for, he added, 'the artillery have worked splendidly and if the enemy does not leave tonight their fight will be continued tomorrow.'

Buller dined contentedly that evening. After all he had dealt with Lyttelton's dangerous commitment on Twin Peaks; he was satisfied that Spion Kop was secure now and could be held next day too, thanks to the guns which by then would be in position. Warren was a shade less happy about the situation.

He was too myopic to have seen the leaderless crowd of soldiers on the near slope of the Kop, swinging anxiously from one side to another in an attempt to escape the shell fire, but some keen-eyed officers on Three Tree Hill had spoken about them to him. At 8 p.m. he had received Coke's defeatist message which had been written two hours earlier, and a little later he was disturbed by Churchill who had come down the hill again and now was haranguing a member of the staff about the necessity of avoiding a second Majuba. Churchill was quite prepared to press his advice on the General, but he was dealt with firmly. 'Who is this man?' Sir Charles shouted when Churchill approached him. 'Take him away. Put him under arrest.'[1]

Fortunately Churchill's friendly staff officer was able to gloss over this awkwardness by suggesting that he go back up the Kop with an assurance for Thorneycroft that help was on its way. Admittedly the mountain battery was resting at the bottom of the hill for some hours in deference to Buller's instructions, but after midnight its guns were to be carried up in sections and Thorneycroft could expect it on the summit well before dawn. There were other encouraging activities to be reported: supplies of food and water as well as ammunition were being organised, while Colonel Sim was parading two hundred men of the Somerset Light Infantry in the darkness before leading them off to improve the entrenchment and to make gun emplacements for the heavy naval guns which were also going up Spion Kop that night.

Yet Warren could not overcome his nagging anxiety, and for the first time we hear of his making the sensible suggestion that he go up to the summit himself and see what the situation was like up there. Then he thought of a better idea: he would send instructions for General Coke to come down and report on conditions at the firing line in person. The order went out and with it Warren ensured that the only man who could have prevented the final consuming tragedy of Spion Kop would spend the next few hours stumbling about in the darkness on the steep hillside, lost and quite unable to control events.

7

WITHDRAWAL

It is a strange commentary on human nature that Colonel Thorneycroft, the man who in Winston Churchill's phrase had fought all day 'like a lion', should at its end have been the man who lost the battle of Spion Kop.

Thorneycroft's nerve snapped soon after 7 in the evening of 24th January, and he gave orders for the hill to be abandoned. It was a sudden resolution, the snap decision of a man who has been tried too far and now is overcome by overpowering depression. Half an hour earlier there had been a lull in the fighting and Thorneycroft had found time to send another situation report to Warren: in it he notified the General of his heavy losses and went on to say, 'if my casualties go on at the present rate I shall barely hold out the night'. In this message, however, there was no suggestion of withdrawing without orders, but merely a warning that unless something was done to assist him and especially to silence the Boer guns, retirement might have to be considered.

It grew dark soon afterwards; the shooting died away; the only sounds on the hilltop were the muffled cries of the wounded and the low exchanges between surviving British officers about dispositions for the night. The 5,000 sorely tried soldiers on the summit could now look forward to rest and relief. Although they were hungry and parched with thirst and their shoulders were aching from the kicks of the fouled rifles they had been firing all day, there was still plenty of fight left in them. As they relaxed and rested a sudden flurry of rifle-fire flared up on their right flank and the darkness of the south-eastern slopes was filled with spurts of flame. It came from no more than a handful of burghers led by Commandant Prinsloo who wished to recover the dead body of his brother before abandoning the Kop; but it sounded and looked far more serious than it really was, and this last gasp of the battle was just enough to break Thorneycroft's spirit. He folded up. His friends later put out the story that Thorneycroft intercepted one of the signals sent by Buller ordering the Rifles to withdraw from Twin Peaks, and that he took it to apply to the whole of the summit.[1] But this attempt at justification for his action is difficult to accept. From the moment of Prinsloo's final attack Thorneycroft acts like a man who admits defeat; he is resolved to get his men off the hill and he will allow no amount of argument to change his decision.

'When night began to close in,' he wrote afterwards, 'I determined to take some steps, and a consultation was held. The officer commanding the Scottish Rifles and Colonel Crofton were both of the opinion that the hill was untenable. I entirely agreed with their view and so I gave the order for the troops to withdarw on to the neck and ridge where the hospital was.'[2]

Here perhaps Thorneycroft is not being perfectly frank. He certainly called a council of his senior officers, but their accounts suggest that it was Thorneycroft, not they, who proposed withdrawal. Thus one of them reports that 'The Commanding Officer merely said: "I should like to ask officers their views. It seems to me impossible to continue to hold on to the hill."'[3] We are told by another of those present that 'some disagreed' with Thorneycroft's opinion that the hill was untenable and that 'words ran high'.[4] In the end the question of retreat or holding on was put to the vote: it seems that the officers were equally divided in the matter until Crofton cast his vote for withdrawal.[5] Colonel Hill was not even present at the council. Despite his belief that he was the senior British officer on the hill he had made no effort to exert his authority over the soldiers fighting on the plateau proper; but he had received a definite order from Coke that the summit must be held through the night, and he would have come out strongly against any suggestion of retreat from Spion Kop. It was therefore most unfortunate then that Hill could not be found in the darkness when the council was assembled.

It is easy to understand the reason for Thorneycroft's break-

Ambulance wagons returning from Spion Kop

The summit: Thursday morning

The main trench after the battle

down: few men could have endured a day like Spion Kop without experiencing a revulsion against the unnecessary suffering and death which had taken place; one eye-witness's account speaks of him staring at the dead men of his unit lying in the trench and muttering over and over again, 'Poor boys, poor boys'.[1]

Nor can one blame him for feeling an overwhelming sense of betrayal: apart from one brief message appointing him to command the troops on the summit, he had heard nothing from Warren all day. For twelve mortal hours he had held a vulnerable position which the military incompetence of his superiors had forced upon him. All that time he had watched the remainder of Buller's army resting below in the valley and apparently making no attempt to relieve the pressure on his own troops, for we must remember that from his position on the summit he had not seen the capture of Twin Peaks by the K.R.R.

Nor had a single word reached him about the arrangements for bringing artillery up Spion Kop during the night; he had not even been told of the preparations being made to supply him with water, food, and ammunition. What he had seen of his senior officers' behaviour had only served to anger and disgust him, and his bitterness increased when he learned that General Coke, his divisional commander, had climbed up to the plateau that afternoon and yet had made no attempt to contact him. Now that the excitement of battle had died out in Thorneycroft it was replaced by a profound depression and a sort of mental palsy. His senses could grasp nothing but the scent of death, the suffering of the wounded, and the horror of a battle which seemed to have reached back in time like a small eternity; and these things had together burned out the belligerency from this exhausted grey-faced man. He was convinced that another day's fighting would mean the annihilation of the surviving soldiers, and he was determined to sacrifice no more of them to his superior officers' incompetence: 'Better six battalions safely off the hill than a mop up in the morning,'[2] he said in answer to protests that he must not abandon Spion Kop, and once made up, his resolve never wavered.

If it is easy to sympathise with Thorneycroft's decision to abandon his position, it is still quite impossible to condone it. In assessing the merits of that decision there are several points for us to consider. One is the fact that the Boers would not have been able to renew the battle for another eight hours at first light, and this gave Thorneycroft plenty of time to acquaint Warren with his intention and allow him to condone or countermand the retreat. Then again (and this strikes one as particularly culpable), Thorneycroft made no attempt to reconnoitre the Boer positions in the dark, let alone probe them with a night attack. Nor did he give any consideration to a compromise solution, such as getting the bulk of his men off the hill in the darkness but at the same time leaving a small holding force on the summit—a course which would have allowed the British to resume the battle next day if the conditions were favourable. This would have had the added advantage of allowing the wounded on the hill top to be succoured during the night. But Thorneycroft ignored their terrible pleadings: in his account he merely explains: 'I was obliged owing to want of stretcher bearers to leave a large number of wounded men on the field.'[1] This was a distressing decision: one suspects that his depression had temporarily unhinged the newly promoted Brigadier-General and had made him exaggerate his losses, for when one officer of the T.M.I. begged permission to remain with a few men on the hill through the night, Thorneycroft assured him that 'there's no regiment left and we shall all have to go down now'.[2]

At 8.15 the leading ranks of the soldiers who had been assembled at the Dressing Station were fallen in again and marched straight down the south-western spur of the Kop. They obeyed their instructions with reluctance: 'What the hell are we leaving the bloody hill for?' was typical of the remarks that a junior commander overhead. They were followed by the remaining soldiers and little parties of those among the wounded who could walk. One wounded officer reported later that he 'started off with the others, supported by a man on either side, but progress in this fashion was so slow that the bottom would never be reached'. Eventually he came to a deserted dressing station, where, he continues, 'many dead were lying about', and these he regarded 'with curious fascination'. A stretcher was found and on this he was put. His two supporters enlisted two others and by these four stalwarts he was borne through the night.[1] Whether by accident or their own design twenty unwounded soldiers were left on the slope near the summit, and in due course they were captured by the Boers.

The first serious opposition to the withdrawal came from Colonel Hill, who was startled to encounter the retreating troops a little below the summit. An angry altercation followed with Thorneycroft, and Hill only gave way after Thorneycroft had assured him that he held the local rank of Brigadier-General and in any case took full responsibility for the retirement. The next attempt to turn Thorneycroft from his purpose came from Winston Churchill who had walked up the Kop again from Three Tree Hill with his messages of assurance concerning Warren's plans for reinforcements during the night. It was about 11.30 that night when Churchill discovered Thorneycroft sitting on the grass in black despair as the soldiers went filing past him. But all Churchill's protests went unheeded and the retreat continued. Half way down the hill Thorneycroft met Colonel Sim leading two hundred men of the Somerset Light Infantry to the plateau. Sim was carrying a written message from Warren urging that the summit be held at all costs. According to an onlooker at this encounter, Thorneycroft seemed 'rather excited'; he said he was unable to read Warren's small handwriting; but when Churchill took the paper and read the message out to him, Thorneycroft retorted: 'I have done all I can and am not going back, and my troops have been ordered to retire.'[2] He then got up and tramped off heavily into the darkness. The company commander of the S.L.I. says that he settled down on the ground to watch him go, and seriously debated with his officers as to whether he should reoccupy the summit with his men; after much discussion he decided that to do so would be to exceed his orders and his company trailed off down the hill behind the others.

The column of men was now approaching General Coke's old command post on the ledge six hundred feet below the plateau, and once again the chances of war seem to have conspired against the British. For a few minutes earlier Coke, the only officer on the hill who possessed the authority to overrule Thorneycroft, had stumbled off to see Warren. He had received the message ordering him to report at Three Tree Hill soon after 9 p.m., and it worried him: he decided to signal Warren's headquarters and explain that it would be very unwise for him to leave his command post at this juncture, but the oil for the signal lamp ran out before more than a few words of his message could be transmitted; after waiting for half an hour while a vain search had been made for more oil Coke decided that he had better comply with his instructions. He was feeling deeply concerned as he started off on the long walk down to Three Tree Hill and he left precise orders with his aide, Captain Phillips, that on no account were the troops to abandon the summit in his absence. It comes as yet another ironic twist on the story of Spion Kop for us to learn that only a few minutes afterwards Phillips received a second signal from Warren to say that, after all, it would do if Coke reported to him in the morning; by then it was too late to recall the General and—a final lapse—Phillips fell asleep despite his anxieties.

Hardly had he dozed off than the head of the retreating column began to tramp past his post, yet two hours went by before the sound of marching feet awakened him. Phillips then grasped the situation at once: this, he told everyone who would listen to him, was an unauthorised withdrawal. There was yet opportunity to retrieve the situation: two battalions under Colonel Cooke still remained on the slopes of the hill and there was plenty of time for them to reoccupy the summit before the Boers discovered it had been abandoned. With some difficulty Phillips persuaded Cooke to halt the rearguard until he had contacted Warren and got him to issue the necessary orders—

but no one had bothered to go on looking for the signal lamp's oil, and three more frantic hours went by while the search was resumed. Only at 2.30 in the morning was the oil found, but now all Phillips' demands that the 'unauthorised withdrawal' be forbidden went unanswered from Three Tree Hill. Time was running out, the troops would be very vulnerable if daylight caught them on the open slopes and Cooke decided that he could wait no longer. The first streaks of dawn were in the sky as the last British soldiers were hustled off the hill. They were followed by a still protesting Captain Phillips.

Nearly all the accounts of the battle of Spion Kop state that there still remained one final and terrible irony in its story, which made a mockery of all the soldiers had endured and suffered that day: they maintain that the Boers had abandoned the summit of Spion Kop long before the British left it, and had accepted total defeat.[1] They state that the Kop remained like an impersonal victor over both sides. But the facts are a little different.

Certainly when darkness came down that Wednesday night most of the Boers were in no better state than the British: they were so numbed with fatigue that few of them had any thoughts except thankfulness at having stayed alive so long and a hope that they would continue to do so. Their feeling of despondency has been well described by a German officer serving with them: 'The day,' he writes, 'gradually reached its close without anybody knowing what was going on or that any change had taken place. We were still expecting some great effort on the part of the enemy which would sweep us off the plateau. With that there was a growing scarcity of ammunition and some of the guns made longish pauses in their firing. Hopes of victory were very faint. The sun sank and a quarter of an hour later it was dark. Firing ceased and the Boers, in spite of orders to stay on the plateau, sneaked away to refresh themselves in the laager. I do not believe there were four untouched Boers left on the hill an hour after sunset. Finally I was left alone, and I followed the example of the others, for I couldn't keep awake any longer and I did not want to be captured.'[1] Raymond

Maxwell, a doctor serving on the Boer side, has this to say in confirmation: 'at dark the burghers decided that they had had enough of it and left the troops in possession of the Kop.'[1]

'That night of the 24th to 25th,' another of their officers remembered, 'was one of confused and chaotic panic which strongly savoured of the beginning of a rout. . . . It was expected that the English would make an attack in force next morning, or perhaps in the night, but the demoralisation was so great that no regular watches were kept all along the line of defence in the proximity of Spion Kop. Here and there, it is true, some determined fellows clubbed together with the resolve to have one more trial the next morning, but there is no doubt that if the British had attacked that night the Federals would have made but poor resistance at the utmost, and their rout would have been a matter of course.'[2]

The 'determined fellows' to which the last writer is referring included Slegtkamp. He stayed at the bottom of the hill through the night, prepared to renew the fight in the morning after he had found his pony.[3] Opperman's commando went one better: its men do not seem to have gone very far from the plateau during the hours of darkness: one of his burghers— H. J. van Wyk—writes that, 'we were on guard, but it was obvious that the enemy were leaving their positions . . . the whole air smelled of human blood and the continuous moaning and groaning of dying English soldiers was indescribable'.[4] W. F. Brink insists too that no less than forty burghers under Sarel Oosthuizen remained near the crest of Spion Kop throughout the night.[5] One of their number rather quaintly remarked of his comrades who had fled that 'their wives and sweethearts were evidently too handsome to be clad in weeds'.[6]

We are on firm ground too when we come to the movements of the Carolina commando after the battle. Many of them admittedly left the hill in the darkness, but a handful of the steadier men remained with Prinsloo when he made the last night attack which so demoralised Thorneycroft. When it was over Prinsloo stationed these burghers just below the eastern rim of the plateau, and then went down the hill to organise food and water for them (it was carried up by coloured servants) and to arrange transport for his wounded. After doing this Prinsloo rode on to his wagon laager to rally those of the Carolina men who had left the field. He is reported to have addressed the waverers with these impassioned words: 'The enemy is retreating faster than you are, and we keep the battlefield. It will be a disgrace afterwards for us who remain in this country to step on the blood of our brave comrades who made such sacrifices earlier this afternoon.'[1] By 10 p.m. he had persuaded about 25 burghers to climb back up the hill with him, and had disposed them in pairs along the brim of the plateau. He did more: he sent two men—Jan Niewoudt and Adriaan Geldenhuys—to follow the retreating soldiers down the hill and to report on their movements at the bottom. After carrying out a brief reconnaissance on the plateau Prinsloo then rejoined his watching burghers. Some of them were finding difficulty in remaining awake: one boy who was only fifteen years old dropped off to sleep; Prinsloo did not reprimand him; instead, he congratulated young de Clercq for being 'the baby of the battle'.[2]

Twin Peaks seems to have remained abandoned by both sides throughout the night, but the newly arrived Standerton commando continued to man the trenches further east and provided a stable hinge on which the Boer line could pivot if the fight were resumed. 'I hope and trust,' its commander signalled Joubert during the night, 'that our Lord will help us and give our burghers strength so that they can hold their positions. Should we hold our positions tonight then I believe that our case has been won.'

Back at his headquarters Botha was unaware of Prinsloo's actions. He had gained the impression that the Kop had been entirely abandoned by the Boers, and it brought a kind of fanaticism to him. Yet this was the inspired fanaticism of a fighter who refuses to accept defeat. Louis Botha was desperately tired, but his clarity of perception, his decisiveness, his energy—and also his good fortune—were unimpaired. He rode again out on to the Rosalie road and halted the wagons that were retreating towards Ladysmith. Deneys Reitz was riding beside one of them: 'just as the foremost wagons moved away,' he writes, 'there came the sound of galloping hooves and a man rode into our midst who shouted for us to halt. I could not see his face in the dark but word went round that it was Louis Botha . . . so eloquent was his appeal that in a few minutes the men were filing off into the darkness to reoccupy their positions.'[1] Instinct had told Botha that he could still win the battle if he could rally only a few score burghers, and his resolution had been fortified by a telegram from Joubert which demanded that an attempt be made to recapture the Kop, 'because it is the key of the matter and has cost too much blood to hand over to the English'. He sent messengers pounding away to Acton Homes to call up comparatively fresh commandos, and then, satisfied that he had done all he could, he lay down and waited for the dawn.

The summit itself was left to the dead and wounded. Those who survived the night spoke later of their experiences there with fearful awe: a terrible stillness, they say, lay over the plateau like a grisly ambience, but every now and again the quiet would be broken by waves of low and dreadful moaning, and the awful dragging sounds of mutilated men as they renewed their search for the water which might have remained in their dead comrades' canteens.

At about midnight a Lieutenant Schwikkard reached the plateau from the British side. He had been sent up the Kop to choose suitable sites for the naval guns which were to come up during the night. Somehow he had missed the retreating troops in the darkness, and now he was startled to discover that both sides had apparently abandoned the positions for which they had fought all day. Prinsloo's pickets must have been lying very low, for Warren reported later that Schwikkard 'ascended Spion Kop by moonlight just after our troops had abandoned it, and entered the Boer lines. Here he found none but killed and wounded except one hospital assistant. There had been a general retirement of the Boers.'[2]

At about this moment General Coke limped thankfully to the place on Three Tree Hill where Warren had set up his headquarters. He was full of complaints at having been made to spend the last few hours stumbling about the hill in the darkness but his indignation gave way to perplexity when he was unable to locate Warren's headquarters wagon: during the afternoon the Boers happened to drop some shells near the wagon, and the General had prudently moved it a few hundred yards away, but without (and by now one has almost come to anticipate the omission) leaving any indication of where he had gone. And so from midnight to 2 a.m. Coke continued his search in the night for his commander's new headquarters. These two hours he wasted cost Warren another opportunity to countermand the withdrawal.

Scarcely had Coke made his report to Warren about the situation on the hill as he had seen it nearly five hours earlier, than Colonel Thorneycroft himself tramped into the faint haze of light cast by hurricane lamps where the two men were standing. Weariness and defeat were glazing his eyes as he announced in flat tones that he had abandoned the Kop.

Even then Phillips was still holding back Cooke and nearly 1,600 soldiers on the spur a few hundred feet below the summit. A signal from Warren could still have resulted in its recapture: there were no more than a handful of Boers about to prevent it and even at this late hour Thorneycroft's decision to evacuate the Kop could have been retrieved. But Warren was stunned by Thorneycroft's report; his only concern now was to shift all responsibility for the débâcle on to someone else's shoulders. As though turning to a prompter for guidance, he tried to send a telegram to Buller asking for advice, but something was always going wrong with his signalling arrangements that day— the wire was down somewhere and the line was dead. Warren then sat down and scribbled out a message for Sir Redvers. He wrote that Thorneycroft had abandoned Spion Kop of his own responsibility, and ended it with a puerile 'can you come at once and decide what to do'.[1] The message was entrusted to a mounted orderly whose instructions were to get it to

Spearman's without delay. The orderly trotted off into the night—and promptly lost his way.

There was movement again on Spion Kop by now. As the soldiers of Cooke's rearguard marched gloomily down its southern slopes they had passed an English doctor leading up a squad of stretcher bearers to attend to the wounded, and these men bravely continued up to the summit. And there were black shadows too moving on the reverse slope: four of Prinsloo's burghers who had remained behind the crest were very cautiously clambering back on to the plateau with the intention of bringing back the body of one of their comrades. They wriggled from one boulder to another. There was no challenge. They raised their heads; they stood up scanning the dark plateau where the gun smoke still rested on the grass; they walked across to the trench, stumbling over inert bodies; then they hurried to the further crest calling out as though to encourage each other, for they were frightened amid such dark scenes of suffering. Apart from the dead and wounded men the summit was deserted. Presently they came upon the two Carolina burghers who had followed the soldiers down the hill and were looking for Prinsloo to report that the battle was won. Soon afterwards they found a group of English stretcher bearers standing appalled near the southern crest. There were hoarse calls of 'hands up' and anxious explanation; then the medical corps men were allowed to attend to the wounded while two of the burghers scrambled down the hill again to tell Botha their news. When they ran up to him he had already collected 450 men at his headquarters and was preparing a counter-attack. There was no need. By 4.30 that morning the Carolina burghers had already occupied the summit and in the first grey light of dawn Commandant Prinsloo was to be seen on the sky line waving his slouch hat on the top of his rifle to call back to the battlefield those Boers he could see retreating in the distance.

It was difficult for these burghers to believe that the British had thrown away their victory. Even as they climbed back up the hill they still suspected a stratagem. But as General

'Marula' Erasmus reported later, 'instead of a great and terrible
fight as we had expected, we found that through God's good-
ness and mercy, the enemy had taken such fear in the night
that they had left their positions and had abandoned a big part
of their dead and wounded'. Something of the burghers'
bewilderment comes out in another report which said: 'Lo! the
English had gone? Was it possible? It might be a trap. But no
it was the truth: no soldiers, with the exception of the harmless
dead and crippled khakis were in sight. The incredible news
spread.'[1] A German officer who realised he had watched the
Boers abandoning the hilltop while the British were preparing
to march down the further side summed up his feelings with a
muttered: 'Wahlhaftig! Dummheit gegen unwissenheit'—
'Truly a case of stupidity against ignorance.'[2]

General Erasmus was the first ranking Boer officer to reach
the summit and he forbade the Red Cross men to remove the
wounded lying there to the dressing station. But as the light
broadened Acting-Commandant-General Louis Botha himself
climbed up the hill. He was horrified by the 'gruesome sicken-
ing hideous picture' of the battlefield, for there were six hundred corpses lying in an area the size of a rugby field and they
'smelled of blood and brains'.[3] The trench presented a particularly dreadful spectacle to Botha who was always sensitive
to human suffering: it was filled with corpses three or four
deep, and in places underneath them wounded men could be
seen moving feebly. But he pulled himself together. His first
action was to inform Joubert by heliograph that his men held
the summit, and he signalled his headquarters near Ladysmith
(whose garrison intercepted and queried this message) that he
was standing among 1,500 dead soldiers.[4] Then he walked to
the southern crest and stood looking at the English camp
below. He saw a scene of great activity. It was a little before
6 a.m., and Buller had just arrived there with his staff.

It had taken the mounted orderly nearly three hours to ride
the eight miles from Warren's headquarters to Spearman's and
not until 5.0 a.m. on the morning of January 25th was Buller
roused to read Sir Charles' timid message. Blinking the sleep

out of his eyes he ordered his horse at once and he was at Three Tree Hill within the hour. He listened to Warren's dismal news with something akin to complacence. It was difficult to analyse all the facets of his mood, but his purest feeling seems to have been a glum satisfaction that Warren, like himself, had failed to defeat the Boers and now no one could possibly expect the newcomer to succeed to his command. Their interview that early morning balanced on the edge of courtesy, as Buller made it clear that he held, not Thorneycroft, but Warren responsible for the débâcle. He promptly removed him from command of the task force. But Buller was not prepared to contest the issue any further; instead he briskly ordered a general retreat to the far side of the Tugela.

By this time even Schalk Burger had got his commando back on to Twin Peaks, and there were more than five hundred Boers on Spion Kop either in defensive positions or searching for the bodies of dead relatives. 'Give us a prayer, dominee,'[1] shouted one of them, and a bearded burgher climbed on to a boulder and launched himself into a sermon. Others, according to the English Dr. Knox, 'assisted in collecting the wounded, and the identification of letters and other contents from the pockets of the dead, which to their credit I must say were handed over to us; others gathered up rifles, bayonets, water bottles, and boots, which they retained. Trophy hunters were cutting off the officers' buttons and badges and this, though galling to us, was in no case carried out with any show of exultancy by the victors.'[2] An English clergyman who climbed up to help the doctor could do very little for some time except repeat, 'My God! What a sight!'[3] Deneys Reitz, long after he had served in the Great War, wrote afterwards, 'there cannot have been many battlefields where there was such an accumulation of horrors within so small a compass',[4] and a Red Cross man remembered that 'an old Boer actually shed tears when he saw the great piles of our dead and wounded and said "poor lads, poor lads".'[5]

The battlefield was indeed a dreadful sight: one Boer journalist counted sixty bodies lying in a short stretch of the main trench and 'entangled as if the dying men had clutched each other in their death struggle . . . dozens of stones were spattered with blood and empty Lee-Metford shells lay about everywhere by the bucketful testifying that the English had spent an enormous amount of ammunition'.[1] Someone else who was impressed by this mournful litter of a battlefield counted forty unopened boxes of ammunition lying behind the trench; another observer was more surprised to see so many empty whisky bottles there and little jars labelled Fortnum and Mason. One burgher wrote home that the plateau was like a ploughed field so numerous were the shell craters on the summit. As he picked his way through the debris a macabre incident occurred nearby when a comrade bent down for a rifle lying on the ground: its dead owner's finger was still curled round the trigger and the gun went off: the inquisitive burgher had the melancholy distinction of being the last man to have been killed in the battle of Spion Kop.[2]

News of the victory sped to the distant Boer camps: 'All morning', one burgher at Ladysmith wrote that night, 'the excitement has been terrible. This evening news came in that for some inscrutable reason the English retired from Spion Kop the night of the fight or early this morning. The burghers are wild with delight. The Boer loss is 200 certain.'[3]

In fact the first official figures released of the Boer loss were somewhat less, they gave their casualties as 58 dead and 140 wounded, but many more burghers are believed to have been killed on and around Spion Kop during the week's operations: on the summit of the Kop today a monument records the names of 106 men who died nearby, and according to one account the number of dead among the Boers exceeded 150. Many of the dead burghers were buried where they fell, but some sixty bodies are known to have been carried down the hill for interment. Casualties were particularly heavy in the Carolina commando: of its 88 men who went into action, 57 were killed or wounded.

The British announced their losses at Spion Kop as 322 men killed, 583 wounded and 300 prisoners of war. According to the Boers this was an under-estimate. Van Enerdingen writes that 'the Boers found between 1,200 and 1,500 dead on the battlefield',[1] and an American, Mr. Webster Davies, said he counted 400 British dead even after 620 soldiers had been buried.[2] Probably the most authoritative figures are those given by Commandant Pretorius who was appointed by Botha to make an accurate count of the killed; he says that he found 650 dead soldiers on Spion Kop, and he estimated that a further 554 men had been wounded and 120 others made prisoners of war.[3]

The Lancashire Fusiliers went into action 800 strong but only 553 survivors answered roll call on Thursday morning,[4] while of the 194 men forming Thorneycroft's Mounted Infantry a mere 72 came down the hill unwounded.

The British casualties appear small when compared with those lost in the far bloodier battles of the Great War, but in 1900 they were considered disastrous, and the publication of the Spion Kop casualty list sent a shudder through the British Empire.

On the summit Botha insisted on making prisoners of Colonel Bloomfield and several other injured British officers. But he allowed the remainder of the wounded men to be taken away by the Medical Corps stretcher bearers and the 25 volunteers of the Natal Ambulance Corps who had followed them up the hill; among the latter was a young Indian lawyer named Mohandas Gandhi who was now making his first appearance on the stage of history. Botha also granted a twenty-four-hour truce to allow the British to bury their dead. On the day following the battle burial parties of soldiers laboriously dug out two large pits; they placed twelve bodies in one and forty-two into the other grave. This was such slow going that the men then simply filled in the eastern half of the trench in which most of the bodies were lying. This part of their work was hurried, and next day the Boers were shocked to see limbs projecting haphazardly from the light covering of earth. That evening the bodies which still remained unburied were looted by Africans. On the 26th and again on the 27th Father Collins led other parties to the summit, and superintended the burial of 84 more corpses; twenty-five bodies were placed in 'a soft piece of ground that seemed like a filled-in trench'.*[1] Of necessity many of them were again 'indecently buried' and the Boers reported later that the graves had been opened at night by robbers.

Even after the British troops had begun their march back to Frere dozens of corpses were still lying exposed on the hill top. Schalk Burger therefore sent a message to Buller proposing that the Boer ambulance men inter those that remained, asking only that the British artillery did not molest them while at work. Buller agreed to the offer and added a shade condescendingly, 'I shall be only too happy to recompense those men you may employ to such an extent as you may think fit and allow me to give.' Not unnaturally Burger took exception to this suggestion.

The Boers' paeans of triumph after their victory were expressed in terms which remind us that, however practical they were, the Bible was their chief support and arbiter in difficulties: the tone was set when one young burgher said to an older companion, 'Uncle, we have won a great victory'; 'No, my child,' answered the other man, 'not we, but God Almighty—and the great pompom.'[2] 'The battle is now over through the mercy of the Lord' Louis Botha telegraphed to Joubert, 'a splendid victory for us . . . it is unbelievable that such a small handful of people could fight the mighty Briton with the help of the Lord for six successive days and thrust them back on the last day with heavy losses.' Commandant Erasmus's report included this passage: 'we cannot be thankful enough to our God and Father for this wonderful victory. The hand of God is also in this as in the other victories he has given us.' Schalk Burger expressed the same appreciation of divine help when he wrote into his account addressed to the Commandant-General, 'we have to thank God, and may I congratulate you and our land and our people. Our burghers have excelled themselves in courage.'

* Almost certainly the trench dug by the Vryheiders above the south-west spur.

The day after the battle Joubert ordered that Spion Kop must be rendered impregnable, and fifty Africans were sent up the hill to help in the digging of field fortifications. They could see Buller's army slowly withdrawing across the Tugela in pouring rain. By the 27th January no soldiers remained on its northern bank. The Boers did not interfere with the retreat. It was said at the time that Botha was afraid that to do so would tempt divine providence too far, and one is reminded here that after his victory at Ladysmith three months earlier Joubert had forbidden pursuit of the beaten English with the remark, 'when God offers you his finger, do not attempt to grasp the whole hand'. The truth was, however, that the Boers were too exhausted even to try to harry the British withdrawal. 'Had we only one good commando', Burger remarked sadly in explanation afterwards, 'we could have done the enemy much damage.'

Buller drew what comfort he could from having extricated his army from an awkward position without having lost 'a pound of stores';[1] he even found it possible to inform London that, while greatly regretting his own casualties, 'we have inflicted on the enemy losses quite as severe as our own. He is thoroughly disheartened while our troops, I am happy and proud to say, are in splendid condition.'[2]

The last part of his message at least was perfectly true. Although Warren was now discredited and some officers were beginning to talk slightingly of Sir 'Reverse' Buller, the troops still retained their faith in their 'bulldog'. To them he implied during a church parade that things would be different in future: after praising the soldiers for their staunch behaviour on Spion Kop, he went on to assure them that 'within a week Ladysmith would be relieved'.[3] This time he said he would lead them in person against the enemy's weakest point—Vaal Krantz—which he had come to realise was the real 'key' to the Boer position. 'May the key fit the lock,' wrote the now thoroughly disillusioned Lieutenant Burne in his diary that night.[4]

8

AFT,ERMATH

The battle smoke had not begun to blow away from Spion Kop before the recriminations began. Warren tells us that early that Thursday morning 'when I met Sir Redvers he used some words in disparagement of General Coke',[1] and that Buller went on to advise him 'that I ought to write a report against General Coke as he had heard that he had been asleep during the action'.[2]

This Warren, to his credit, declined to do, and since Buller could scarcely blame Thorneycroft—his own nominee as fighting commander—for the disaster, it seemed that he would have to make Warren its scapegoat.   One can see the way in which his mind was working that first morning after the battle, for as Buller rode away from Spion Kop he remarked to Dundonald, 'I blame myself for not controlling Sir Charles Warren, but he was sent out after Colenso under such auspices that I did not like to interfere with him'.[3] Then at noon that same day, the 25th January, Buller settled down in his tent and composed a message for immediate transmission to London. It read: 'Warren's garrison, I am sorry to say, I find in the morning, had in the night abandoned Spion Kop.'[4] It reached London in time for the next day's late editions, and though it sounded as if it had been written more in sorrow than in anger, it squarely laid the blame for the débâcle on Warren's shoulders. In the morning all the newspapers headlined the defeat and Warren's implied responsibility for it.

But there was no unanimity among the soldiers in South Africa about this inculpation. Buller came in for a good deal of criticism too: Lyttelton, for instance, wrote home that 'I have lost all confidence in Buller as a General and I am sure he had done so himself';[5] Lord Roberts, while allowing that Thorneycroft's withdrawal was 'wholly inexcusable' and that he considered it reprehensible that Warren had never visited the summit during the battle, maintained that 'the chief fault lay in the disinclination of the officer in supreme command to assert his authority and see that what he thought best was done'.[1] Esher's criticism was even more to the point: 'Buller has shown no grip,' he said. 'He eats too much.'

While the first verbal volleys were being fired of an argument that would soon stir all England, Buller's disconsolate army was retreating in pouring rain across the Tugela. The soldiers thought it bad enough to have been beaten but it was doubly distressing for the survivors of the battle to realise that a splendid tactical opportunity had been thrown away and all their courage and endurance wasted. 'The army was irritated,' wrote Churchill, 'by the feeling that it had made sacrifices for nothing. It was puzzled and disappointed by a failure which it did not admit nor understand.'[2] The men's temper was not improved when they looked back at the hill and watched groups of Boers moving about on its summit and once they saw a girl there in a piqué dress who carried a red parasol; the scene of their agony, it appeared, had become a tourist attraction.

Only Warren seemed undismayed by the defeat; he felt thoroughly satisfied with the way he had conducted the action, and he complacently informed a young officer 'that the Boers had had a severe knock at Spion Kop and were ready to run on seeing British bayonets'. Admittedly he had lost the battle but all responsibility for this devolved, he thought, upon Thorneycroft; and he pointedly quoted Lord Wolseley's aphorism that 'an officer in command who abandoned the defence of a post, as long as one third of his garrison remains effective, deserves to be shot'.[3] And now that the army was moving through sodden country again he could indulge himself in his 'old capacity as leader or ganger': 'I started as my first concern,' he tells us with his old bounciness, on 'the regulation of all traffic on the road leading to Potgieter's'.[4]

On the 30th January, having chewed over in his mind the events of the past week, Sir Redvers Buller settled down to write his despatch on the Spion Kop operations for the War Office. He was at pains to emphasise his detachment from all responsibility for the defeat and pointed again to the real culprit by maintaining that 'Warren mixed up all the brigades, and the position he held was dangerously insecure'. But the most damaging criticism of his second-in-command only appeared in that part of the despatch which he carefully labelled 'not necessarily for publication'; in this he wrote that Warren 'seems to me to be a man who can do well what he can do himself but he cannot command, as he can use neither his staff nor subordinates. I can never employ him again on an independent command.'[1]

The Spion Kop despatch caused a tremendous stir in London. The Cabinet forbade the publication of its 'secret' section but the edited portion that did appear only served to arouse the suspicion that something was being kept back from the public. 'Whatever else our generals can do,' Chamberlain told his wife, 'they cannot write despatches',[2] while someone else jibed that the British leaders 'seem unable either to win victories or give intelligent accounts of their defeat'.[3] The Cabinet's sense of humiliated frustration was only increased by the offers of help which inundated it: the Kaiser offered his services as unofficial military adviser; the Italian Government came up with a suggestion that it send troops to relieve the British forces in Egypt so that they might proceed to the front; while the Sultan of Turkey even proposed that his own army take the field against the Boers in place of the defeated British.

The check at Spion Kop at first temporarily deflated Buller, and he told Lyttelton that he was now 'at his wits' end' about the way in which Ladysmith might be relieved.[4] But the completion of his task of placing the blame for his own shortcomings on his scapegoats seemed to have a tonic effect. Lord Roberts on the western front by now was reinforcing Methuen's army outside Kimberley preparatory to making his main thrust into the Orange Free State and he advised Buller to make no more attempts on the Tugela line until his own army was in a position to support him. But Buller was unprepared to take this advice. 'Delay is objectionable', he wired back to

Roberts, and went on to say that he intended 'using a new drift (Munger's Drift) just discovered which makes all the difference by enabling me to reach a position hitherto considered inaccessible'.[1] He told him that he was accordingly going to storm the heights at a defile running below a hill named Vaal Krantz, and added, 'I feel fairly confident of success this time'.

For Vaal Krantz was the 'key' to Ladysmith about which he had spoken to his troops, and there was some reason for his confidence. Drafts had more than made up for his losses at Spion Kop, and that first week in February his striking force numbered 21,000 men and 66 guns. Many of the Boers opposed to him had taken themselves off on leave and there were scarcely more than 4,000 burghers in the trenches along the heights. Probably they had less than 400 men and six guns available to defend Vaal Krantz itself.

Moreover, Buller's plan of attack was a good one. He intended to seize the flat-topped Vaal Krantz, mount guns on it (this seemed perfectly feasible since a helpful local farmer had said that the hill was an exact replica of Swartz Kop, and the sappers had already succeeded in hauling guns up there) and so dominate the defile leading to the Ladysmith plain.

Sir Redvers got Warren out of harm's way by giving him the inglorious task of making a demonstration before the real attack went in; perhaps this was wise since Warren did not think very highly of Buller's new scheme: 'the place we are going to assault', he confided to his wife in a pessimistic letter home, 'is the most difficult I have ever seen. It will take a Higher Hand to get us through, and something more like a miracle than generally occurs.'[2]

In this opinion he was perfectly correct for once. The battle of Vaal Krantz turned out to be Spion Kop in miniature: the hill was stormed on the 5th February; but now the soldiers were pinned down on its summit by accurate cannon fire and Sir Redvers' nerve began to waver. 'Then,' writes Lyttelton, 'as had become his habit, Buller began to shilly-shally.'[3] He telegraphed Roberts that to continue the attack might cost two or three thousand casualties, and in another attempt to shift responsibility, he asked 'do you think the chance of relieving Ladysmith worth the risk?'[1] Roberts replied that he thought it was, but Buller after more time for reflection did not agree and on the 7th he retired the army back to the south side of the Tugela. He again obtained comfort in the efficiency with which the retreat was conducted; in a happy mood he told a member of his staff that it had gone 'uncommonly well' and was only slightly put out by the tactless reply of 'yessir, you've practised it twice'.[2] The *Times History* sums up the battle of Vaal Krantz very harshly as 'one of the feeblest performances in the history of war'.[3]

Buller's third defeat at Botha's hands was at least far less costly than those at Colenso and Spion Kop, and by now in any case it did not matter very much. For the tide of war in South Africa was beginning to turn dramatically. Lord Roberts' offensive relieved Kimberley and led to the invasion of the Free State and the Transvaal.

But Buller still intended to go on 'pegging away' at the Tugela defences: 'My plan', he heliographed to Sir George White in Ladysmith after Vaal Krantz, 'is to slip back to Chieveley' and renew the attack; he added hopefully, 'Keep it dark',[4] and then a little plaintively, 'can you think of anything better?' White probably could have thought of something better but if he bothered to communicate his opinion to Buller's headquarters it was too late, for the General had already 'slipped back' to Chieveley without waiting for a reply. He was there on the 9th February and full now of his old scheme of breaking through at Colenso before the Boers could reoccupy the trenches there in strength. He was stunned, however, to find that they had forestalled him: 'they do in six hours and 7 miles', he wailed to Roberts, 'what takes me three days and 26 miles.'[5] He went on to ask Lord Roberts for more troops; this drew a withering comment from Sir Charles Warren to whom he had unwisely shown his request, and it still has the power to surprise us: 'you have stated in your recent telegram', Warren told him, 'that you cannot relieve Ladysmith without considerable reinforcements. In this I disagree with you; you have not given a fair trial to my methods.'[1]

Although it took him more than four months to brush aside an enemy less that a quarter of his strength, the Boer line below Colenso did begin to crumple up after a new attack towards Hlangwane had been made; on 28th February 1900 Lord Dundonald led the cavalry brigade into Ladysmith and the 113-day siege was over. For a moment there was a good chance of destroying the Boer army in Natal but Buller obstinately refused to follow up his opportunity. He said he would not risk losing 'a single man' to capture the entire Boer transport and camp, and so Botha was allowed to withdraw his army intact: 'I cannot think of that day even now,' à Court was to write later, 'without rage',[2] while Lyttelton commented that 'few commanders have so wantonly thrown away so great an opportunity'.[3] Buller, however, enjoyed himself making a ceremonial entry into Ladysmith with 20,000 troops whose physical condition poignantly contrasted with that of the garrison. The triumph was accordingly somewhat marred by accusations of bad taste; Colonel Sim was speaking for many when he remarked that this entry was 'one of the most mournful pageants that could have been devised by idiotic generals'.[4] Buller was feeling annoyed that day with Sir George White who had tactlessly mustered a column of half-dead men on foundered horses from the Ladysmith garrison to pursue the Boers. And though all England thrilled over an imaginative artist's depiction of the handclasps exchanged by the two generals over the withers of their horses (the picture was unashamedly based on the more famous painting of Blücher and Wellington after Waterloo), in fact Buller looked the other way when he rode past General White standing at the salute outside Ladysmith Town Hall. 'Buller was very rude to Sir George,' Ian Hamilton wrote a few days later to Lord Roberts, 'and spoke in the vilest way of you and Kitchener, whom he appears to dislike and to attribute dishonest motives.'[5] But then of course Hamilton, like most of the other officers in Ladysmith was completely disillusioned by Buller; he even wrote home to a friendly politician that *'Buller is no use*. It is a question of life or death for ourselves here as well as of the Empire in general, and I write to beg you to use all your influence to get the man recalled before he does more mischief.'[1]

The war was by no means over with the relief of Ladysmith and Roberts' capture of Pretoria. It still had two long years to run, and by the time peace came, Louis Botha was the only one of the three chief actors of the Spion Kop drama still in the field. General Warren was the first to go: he was got out of the way by a posting to the relatively untroubled province of Griqualand West. Landsdowne at the War Office was delighted to hear of his move: 'It struck me,' he wrote to Roberts, 'that after what had passed, he and Buller could not with advantage remain together.'[2] Warren felt the same way. On 6th March 1900, only a few days after Ladysmith's relief, he tells us that he 'took leave of General Buller and in a very joyful frame of mind proceeded south'[3] with his staff. On the way to Durban he decided to make a pilgrimage to Spion Kop, and attend a service to be held at a mass grave on the banks of the Tugela. But as always at Spion Kop his arrangements went sadly astray and in a manner which cannot be followed better than in Warren's own account: 'On arrival at the Tugela north of Mount Alice,' he writes, 'it was found that the grave to be blessed was on the south side and we were on the north side. Here was a dilemma. The Tugela was rather in flood.' The situation, however, was saved, though in a somewhat inde-corous manner, when the priest and acolyte stripped and swam the river. Warren in his account goes on to say that he watched 'Father Collins in his buff, covered only by very light canon-icals and carrying some religious vessel, while his orderly marched behind stark naked but with great dignity. Thus the ceremony was carried through—possibly one of the most impressive ceremonies I have ever witnessed—and we from our side of the river took part in it. It was a blazing hot day and I thought that the orderly's back would be one long blister, but he would not allow that he had felt any discomfort.'[4]

After the service Warren trudged up Spion Kop for the first

time and thought 'it did not seem much of a hill. . . . General Coke was with me and we came to the conclusion that it ought not to have been abandoned. This is still an open question, but I felt that even so we ought to have retaken it next day.' Clearly Warren regarded Buller and Thorneycroft as still being the chief culprits for the defeat there.

At Durban a few days later Warren was filled with scandalised indignation when he found orders telling him to return to Ladysmith. He remained there only one week, however, leaving after a blazing row with Buller. 'He was at that time smarting at Lord Roberts' rebuffs about Spion Kop', Warren explains, 'and he made out that it was all my fault . . . we both spoke in very strong terms.'[1] The terms would have been even stronger if Sir Charles had known of Buller's comments in both his published and 'secret' despatches about his conduct of the operation.

Warren was brought back to England four months later and was heard to refer to himself then as 'the scapegoat-in-chief of the army in South Africa'.[2]

Only now did he read the first of Buller's Spion Kop despatches and he naturally deeply resented the savage attack on his generalship. Since further military glory was now clearly denied him, Warren took refuge in reminiscence, and 1902 saw the publication of *On the Veldt in the Seventies* in which he expanded on earlier triumphs in Bechuanaland. The publication of the Spion Kop 'secret' despatches of course added fuel to his smouldering wrath, but a candid friend advised him to 'grin and bear it', and 'to begin all over again in some other line, and show the world you are not the idiot Buller makes you out to be'.[3]

The line Warren chose was 'to make order out of the confused chaos of weights and measures and also to find out what's the matter with the world's position—as no astronomers as yet, have been able to find any law for the position of the planets.' His efforts to do so resulted in the publication of *The Ancient Cubit and our weights and measures* and *Early weights and Measures of Mankind*.[4]

Sir Charles was nothing if not versatile; he tells us he next made the discovery that 'boys are more difficult to govern than men are so I determined to go in for education for boys'.[1] With praiseworthy energy he superintended a Sunday School class and raised a unit of the Church Lads' Brigade in Ramsgate; a few years later he decided to devote his time to the new Scout movement and the First Ramsgate ('Sir Charles Warren's Own') Boy Scout Troop came into being. The interest continued. We have an engaging vignette of the aged Sir Charles in Scout uniform assisting the Archbishop of Canterbury at some stone-laying ceremony as late as 1920, and still he continued to live on, all rancour and spleen drained out of him, a dear old man seeking always to help young people. Sir Charles Warren died in 1927 in his 87th year.

By then Louis Botha had been dead for over eight years. After Joubert's death he had become the Boer Commander-in-Chief and won many fresh military laurels during the guerrilla phase of the Anglo-Boer War, developing his instinctive tactical genius and ability to anticipate events. Botha fought many actions after Spion Kop and with the exception of the Bergendal affair he never lost a single one of them. He had the unusual experience of fighting a skirmish across one of his own farms, and three weeks later at Bakenlaagte gained a minor triumph which was typical of many, when at the head of 1,000 burghers he routed 1,600 soldiers, killing and wounding 600 and capturing 200 for the loss of 14 Boers killed and 48 wounded. In the end Great Britain deployed 450,000 soldiers in South Africa against the Boers. When peace came back to the veld in 1902 Botha travelled to England to raise money for the reconstruction of his country and he was surprised to receive a hero's welcome there. He responded by labouring for conciliation between Boer and Briton in South Africa. That work bore fruit in 1910 when Louis Botha became the first Prime Minister of the Union of South Africa. Four years later he took his country into the Great War on England's side and cleared South-West Africa of Germans. Louis Botha's enormous career ended at the age of 57; he left behind him the memory of a born soldier who yet was always filled with compassion for others' sufferings; General Smuts was not exaggerating when he wrote of his friend that 'He combined the strength of a man with the sensitiveness of a woman', and over Botha's grave Smuts burst out with 'He was the cleanest, sweetest soul of all the land—of all my days.'[1]

Buller died in 1908. He had been recalled from South Africa towards the end of 1900 following his signal failure to press his advantage against the demoralised Boers after the relief of Ladysmith. His indecisiveness then had led Lord Lansdowne to believe that the General's mind was 'unhinged', while Lyttelton wryly said that his handling of the Natal operation resembled 'the disastrous defeats' suffered by McDowell, McClellan, Pope, Burnside, and Hooker during the early stages of the American Civil War except that 'the difference was that all of these, except McClellan, were promptly relieved of their commands after one failure'.[2] Dundonald made no bones about telling Buller to his face that he had changed from the man he was, at which Buller tearfully agreed and cried, 'It is true, and what changed me was the indoor life at that cursed War Office, those long hours, day after day, without exercise, for I used to work there long after the others had gone.'[3]

In England Buller was well received by the public but was disappointed to be fobbed off with a mere G.C.M.G., whereas Lord Roberts received another step in the peerage. He was shocked, too, to discover that Wolseley had turned against him, and had written of his old protégé that he was 'thoroughly disappointed in him for he had not shown any of the characteristics I attributed to him; no military genius, no firmness, not even the obstinacy which I thought he possessed when I discovered him. He seems dazed and dumbfounded.'

Buller, however, was restored to the Aldershot command, the country's most important military training centre, but memories of Spion Kop continued to haunt him. The press was filled with criticism of his tactics during the campaign and with rumours that his nerve had so snapped after Colenso that he had advised Sir George White to surrender Ladysmith. These rumours were perfectly true, of course, but in the October of 1901 Buller could stand them no longer. He answered his critics in a speech at the end of a convivial regimental luncheon; fortified perhaps by too much champagne and with Dunmore quite forgotten he regaled his audience with some absurd story about an encounter with a Transvaal spy at Aldershot;[1] he then proceeded to explain away the unfortunate invitation to General White to surrender Ladysmith which he said he had 'spatchcocked' into a message after the battle of Colenso;[2] he had done so, he asserted, to relieve White of responsibility and shame if he were obliged to capitulate. It was a particularly lame excuse and no one believed it. The authorities moreover regarded the speech as a breach of discipline; one feels that they welcomed the opportunity it gave them of getting rid of Buller; and he was removed from his military command at Aldershot. By now Buller had become something of a joke in military circles and Saki lampooned the fallen idol as Humpty Dumpty in a parody 'Alice in Westminster' which began:

> I sent a message to the White
> To tell him—if you must, you might
> But then, I said, you p'raps might not
> (The weather was extremely hot)
> This query, too, I spatchcock-slid
> How would you do it if you did?
> I do not know, I rather thought——
> And then I wondered if I ought.[3]

Sir Redvers now disappeared into the comfortable obscurity of his Devonshire estate, where if he was a little old for hunting he could still indulge his passion for growing apples, but still he was not allowed to forget Spion Kop. That same year Mr. L. S. Amery began to write his history of the Boer War in which, because he believed it to be in the national interest, he criticised Buller's conduct of the Natal campaign very severely. The whole issue was revived in 1902 when the 'secret' despatch on Spion Kop was printed, and the public was entertained by an acrimonious correspondence between Sir Redvers and Mr. A. J. Balfour. In it, Buller 'strenuously denied that he was in command of the Spion Kop operations, even going so far as to assert repeatedly that he had not been present at them or witnessed them';[1] this assertion Balfour promptly pointed out was palpably untrue since on the 16th of January 1900 Buller had ordered Warren to cross the Tugela, on the 21st he gave personal directions regarding the siting of the British artillery, on the 22nd he agreed to the attempt on Spion Kop, and next day selected Woodgate as its commander; finally Buller was reminded that it was he who had suggested the replacement of Crofton by Thorneycroft as commander on the summit, and that he had personally controlled the movements of Lyttelton's troops against Twin Peaks.

In 1903 all the old wounds were reopened once more when Buller appeared before a Royal Commission examining the military conduct of the war. Lord Esher felt his sympathy reaching out to the General after listening to him trying to explain away his mistakes, and he reported to King Edward VII that 'in spite of his great failings he is a very human figure. Unpleasing in appearance, with no command of temper, he is nevertheless a man of strong sympathies and generous impulses.'

Perhaps that was as fair a summing-up of General Buller's character as it is possible to make, and it is comforting to know that right up to his death Sir Redvers never lost the regard and respect of the soldiers he had commanded nor of the Devonshire people among whom he lived. His admirers' efforts succeeded in converting him into a kind of military Tichborne claimant, and before his death Buller experienced the rare satisfaction of having a statue of himself erected at Exeter on whose base was inscribed 'He saved Natal'.

At bottom, Buller had been defeated at Spion Kop because his will to victory was weaker by far than that of Louis Botha. Yet many other factors and accidents had contributed to that defeat—the contemporary training of the regular British army which had made its officers afraid to take bold decisions, the failure of the English commanders in modern warfare which was so abject that, among the Boers, it was said to be a capital offence to shoot at an English general, the bad marksmanship of the infantry, Buller's own abdication from command which had resulted in withdrawing the linchpin of the military framework during battle, the failure to take sandbags up Spion Kop, the wrong siting of the trench on its summit, the omission to reconnoitre the plateau, the inadequacy of the British artillery and the surprising effectiveness of the Boers', the breakdown of the army's communications, the absurd confusion about the command of the British troops on the hill, and Coke's fatuous two-hour search in the darkness for Warren's headquarters—all these unexpected developments had added up to a recipe for defeat.

. . . Yet not for disaster. The Boers had expected Spion Kop to be a second Majuba which would compel Great Britain to sue for peace as she had done in 1881. But her army in Natal still lived and moved after the battle. The sheer grit of the ordinary soldiers in Buller's command allowed them to redeem the crass ineptitude of their commanders; their willingness to go on fighting after the three humiliating defeats on the Tugela enabled Lord Roberts to roll up the Boer flank in the Orange Free State and ensure ultimate victory.

And the horrible mismanagement of the Spion Kop battle paid off a dividend of another kind: it pricked the reputations of England's most renowned generals and provided the War Office in London with the stimulus to undertake the complete reform of the British military machine. Nothing was quite the same at Whitehall after Spion Kop, and although the old Queen still had a year to live, the Victorian age ended for Britain when a dejected Thorneycroft tramped heavily down Spion Kop in defeat. Pondering over the débâcle L. S. Amery wrote that it 'left on my mind an ineffaceable impression of the incapacity of our senior officers . . . and of the urgent need of complete military reform of the army from top to bottom'.[1] Thanks to his energy the stubborn supporters of the out-of-date at the War Office were swept away and the whole phalanx of professional conservatism dispersed. That the necessary reforms were effected during the next decade and that an army able to meet more perilous demands took the field in 1914 is proof that the soldiers' sacrifices on Spion Kop fourteen years earlier had not been entirely wasted.

APPENDIX

It is of some interest to consider the later careers of the lesser participants in the Spion Kop battle. Those of Winston Churchill and Mahatma Gandhi are too well known to require attention here, while the career of Thorneycroft was so marred by the battle that he died comparatively unknown in 1931.

Commandant Prinsloo was killed in action later in 1900. He had been slightly wounded in the head during the fighting on Spion Kop, but after a period in hospital he resumed command of the Carolina commando. On 7th November he led it to attack a British column under General Smith-Dorrien just outside Belfast in the Transvaal. Prinsloo was shot dead during the action which followed within sight of his wife and family. He was buried on the field and in 1926 a monument which owed much to Smith-Dorrien's generosity was raised to his memory over the grave. Every year on the anniversary of Prinsloo's death a group of burghers gather there to stand for a few moments in silent tribute to one of the few men who took away from Spion Kop a better reputation than he had brought to it.

Lyttelton did well during the Boer War and when peace returned to the veld he succeeded Lord Kitchener as Commander-in-Chief, South Africa. He soon established friendly relations with the Boer generals and played a large part in reconciling the differences between Great Britain and the two Afrikaner republics. Lyttelton died full of years and honours as Governor of the Royal Hospital, Chelsea.

His old Brigade Major, Henry Wilson, rose to the rank of Field-Marshal and became Chief of the Imperial General Staff during the 1914–18 war. His promotion was owed to ability and influential patronage rather than to his embarrassingly pungent personality. Wilson was more of a politician than a soldier; he was shot dead by Sinn Feiners on the doorstep of his London home in 1922.

Commandant 'Rooi Daniel' Opperman remained in the field throughout the Boer War and was one of the Transvaal delegates when the Peace of Vereeniging was signed in 1902. He remained faithful to the British connection during the Transvaal and Free State rebellion of 1914, and fought under Botha in crushing it. Opperman became a Senator and died in 1927.

à Court left the army soon after the relief of Ladysmith as the result of some indiscretion. Although Lord Roberts favoured his reinstatement King Edward VII refused to sanction it. à Court, who had changed his name to Repington, revenged himself at the time when the King sent for Asquith to kiss hands at Biarritz, by writing a venomous article of criticism about this unconstitutional behaviour. Repington is now best remembered as an influential military correspondent of *The Times*.

One never knows quite what to make of Dundonald: he emerges from the official reports of the Tugela campaign as a dashing cavalry leader who was thwarted time and time again by his bumbling superior officers, yet the contemporary accounts of his subordinates have little good to say about this man, and paint him as a puffed up incompetent. Dundonald came of a noble family which included its fair number of eccentrics. Together with his title he had come into an unusual inheritance which kept him awake on the night after the battle on Spion Kop—secret plans for making smoke screens to cover naval attacks. 'I also kept turning over in my mind', he writes in his autobiography, 'whether I should not go to see Sir Redvers Buller with the object of revealing to him the secret plans of my grandfather, Admiral Lord Dundonald, which had been handed to my keeping by Lord Playfair under solemn promise that they would only be revealed in the event of a national emergency. In my mind's eye I saw the great banks of smoke, producing an atmosphere—to use the words of the plans—"dark as the darkest night"; then I thought of this same atmosphere impregnated with sulphur. I saw the line of Boer riflemen in their trenches, waiting for our men, with Mausers useless, for those that held them could not see . . . but I restrained myself and kept the secret.'[1]

Dundonald says he was one of the first men into Ladysmith when the siege was raised (an assertion disputed by his subordinates). From South Africa he went to Canada as commander of the militia, but was quickly recalled after quarrelling with the local politicians. He revealed his famous secret to the War Office during the Kaiser's War; his smoke screens were successfully used on the Western Front, and Lord Dundonald has gone down in history as one of the originators of chemical warfare.

*

When a memorial service was held on Spion Kop in 1964 it was attended by 23 veterans of the battle. Since then their number has steadily decreased and today only the Kop and its surroundings remain as they were in 1900.

A large cross has been set up on Mount Alice to mark the spot from which Sir Redvers Buller watched the fighting on the other side of the valley. The air here is still filled with the peaceful sounds of doves just as it was when the British army's tents were scattered among the thorn trees. And the same panorama unfolds itself before Mount Alice which Buller peered at through his glass, but the domed crest of Spion Kop is notched now with memorials and cenotaphs scattered across this 'acre of massacre' where so many men died.

Coming to the Tugela it is still possible to see where General Warren's engineers cut their roadways down to the pontoon bridges across which the soldiers marched to their bungled battle with the Boers. But another generation of engineers is at work close by and soon the waters of an enormous dam will fill the valley, obliterating its old landmarks, and lapping right up to Three Tree Hill itself. Standing today on this hill at the old site of Strike Force Headquarters, it is easy to understand why Warren's tactical control of the battle erred so badly, for Aloe Knoll and Twin Peaks are out of sight, hidden behind the western shoulder of Spion Kop.

A visitor will find it easier to ascend the Kop on the Boer side rather than from the south. A dirt road leads him past the hillock on which Louis Botha pitched his tent before the battle, and it is not difficult to visualise him running down to the Rosalie road to rally his retreating burghers. The track then leads up and around Conical Hill and so to the plateau itself. There the visitor finds himself surrounded by graves and obelisks. Even if alone he will not feel lonely; rather he will experience a strange sensation of being watched wherever he may walk on this confined and affecting battle-field, watched without acrimony or inquisitiveness, but rather with intentness and compassion.

The distant line of the Drakensberg mountains stretches in a great arc across the western horizon, and one can recognise the Sentinel at Mont-aux-Sources where the Tugela begins, and the elongated mass of Tintwa shaped like the profile of Dundonald's face, and Giant's Castle, and a score of other peaks whose splendour becomes the valour of the dead they watch. Yet whatever the mountains' magnificence, the eye is brought back time and again to the trench which the soldiers dug along the plateau one misty morning, and which serves them as a grave. Round black stones from the summit have been piled now on top of this trench-grave to spare it from pillagers, and beside it among the boulders grows the tufted coarse grass which is mentioned in nearly all contemporary accounts of the battle; green in summer, it turns straw coloured with the approach of winter; but after frost the grass takes on a reddish tinge as though mindful of all the life blood which stained it at the beginning of the century.

BIBLIOGRAPHY

(The following books and articles are those referred to in the reference notes)

A. 1. *Archives Year Book of S.A. History.* 23rd year, vol 2, Govt Printer, 1961.
   2. Amery, L. S. *The Times History of the War in South Africa,* vols 2 & 3. Lond. Sampson Low, Marston. 1902–5.
   3. Amery, L. S. *My political life.* Lond., Hutchinson, 1953.

B. 1. Birdwood, W. R. *Lord Birdwood. Khaki and Gown: an Autobiography.* Lond., Ward, Lock. 1941.
   2. Bul, *pseud.* 'The battle of Spioenkop' in *Commando,* Jan. & Feb. 1965.
   3. Burleigh, B. *The Natal Campaign.* Lond., Bell, 1900.
   4. Burne, R. N. *With the Naval Brigade in Natal 1899–1900.* Lond., Arnold, 1902.

C. 1. Caldwell, T. C. *The Anglo-Boer War.* Boston, D. C. Heath, 1965.
   2. Capstickdale, L. 'Spion Kop—Hill of valour' in *South African Panorama,* Vol. 9, 10 September 1964.
   3. Celliers, J. H. 'Die Slag van Spioenkop' in *S.A. Archives Year Book* 1960, part 2.
   4. Churchill, W. S. *London to Ladysmith,* Lond., Longmans, Green, 1900.
   5. Creswicke, L. *South Africa and the Transvaal War,* vol. 3. Edinburgh, T. C. & E. C. Jack, 1900.

D. 1. De Clercq, G. Private papers in possession of the author.
   2. Defender, *pseud. Sir Charles Warren and Spion Kop.* Lond., Smith, Elder, 1902.
   3. Dundonald, D. M. B. G., *Lord Dundonald. My army life.* Lond., Edward Arnold, 1926.

E. 1. Engelenburg, F. V. *General Louis Botha.* Pretoria, J. L. Van Schaik, 1929.

F. 1. Fitzpatrick, Sir J. *South African Memories*. Lond., Cassell, 1932.

G. 1. Great General Staff, Berlin. *The War in South Africa*. Lond., Murray, 1906.

H. 1. Hamilton, I. B. M. *The happy warrior*. Lond., Cassell, 1966.
   2. Headlam, C. (ed). *The Milner Papers,* vol 2. Lond., Cassell, 1933.
   3. Holt, E. *The Boer War*. Lond., Putnam, 1958.

J. 1. Jerrold, W. *Sir Redvers Buller, V.C.* Lond., S. W. Partridge, 1900.
   2. *Journal of the Diehards,* September 1947.

K. 1. Kearsey, A. H. C. *War Record of the York and Lancaster Regiment*. Lond., Bell, 1903.
   2. Knox, E. B. *Buller's Campaign*. Lond., R. Brimley Johnson, 1902.
   3. Kruger, R. *Goodbye Dolly Gray*. Lond., Cassell, 1959.

L. 1. Lehman, J. *All Sir Garnet*. Lond., Cape, 1964.
   2. Lemmer, N. M. *Die Slag van Spioenkop*. Memorial Programme, 1964.

M. 1. Maurice, Sir F. *History of the war in South Africa*. Lond., Hurst & Blackett, 1907.
   2. Melville, C. H. *Life of the Right Hon. Sir Redvers Buller*. 2 v. Lond., Edward Arnold, 1923.
   3. Morris, D. R. *The washing of the spears*. N.Y., Simon & Schuster, 1965.
   4. Mostert, D. *Slegtkamp van Spionkop*. Cape Town, Nasionale Pers. Beperk, 1935.

O. 1. Oppenheim, L. 'Thorneycroft's Mounted Infantry on Spion Kop' in *Nineteenth Century,* Jan. 1901.

P. 1. Park-Gray, W. Letter to Mr. G. Mackenzie in the possession of Dr. R. E. Stevenson.
   2. Pemberton, W. B. *Battles of the Boer War*. Lond., Batsford, 1964.

R. 1. Reitz, D. *Commando*. Lond., Faber, 1929.
   2. Repington, C. à C. *Vestigia*. Lond., Constable, 1919.

S. 1. Spender, H. *General Botha*. Lond., Constable, 1916.
   2. Standertonner, *pseud.* 'Hendrik Prinsloo'. in *Die Huisgenoot,* 4 Dec. 1936.
   3. Symons, J. *Buller's Campaign*. Lond., Cresset P., 1963.

U. 1. *United Services Magazine,* Feb., 1902.

V. 1. Villebois-Mareuil, Col. de, *War Notes*. Lond., A. & C. Black, 1902.

W. 1. Warren, Sir C., *On the veldt in the seventies*. Lond., Isbister, 1902.
   2. Watkins-Pitchford, H. *Besieged in Ladysmith,* Pietermaritzburg, Shuter & Shooter, 1964.
   3. Williams, W. W. *The life of General Sir Charles Warren*. Oxford, Blackwell, 1941.
   4. Wilson, H. W. *With the flag to Pretoria*. Lond., Harmsworth, 1900.

REFERENCES

These refer to the titles in the Bibliography)

PAGE	REF. NO.	SOURCE	PAGE	REF. NO.	SOURCE
3	1	J1,228	20	3	R2,201
4	1	J1,240	21	1	A2,II,142
	2	J1,240	25	1	B4,13
	3	R2,194		2	S3,148
	4	H2,8		3	B3,150
8	1	J1	26	1	G1,119
9	1	S3		2	B3,235
	2	V2,313		2	R2,211
	3	M2,I,16		3	M2,II,72
	4	M2,I,16	27	1	M2,II,77
10	1	M2,II,20	28	1	M2,II,94
	2	M1,261		2	H2,47
	3	M2,II,262		3	M2,II,91
11	1	L1,346	30	1	L3,211
	2	L1,287		2	H2,28
	3	J1,228		3	L3,214
	4	J1,228		4	M2,II,113
12	1	M1,261		5	W3,260
	2	P2,92		6	A3,154
	3	S3,91		7	He,155
	4	H1,145		7	M2,II,120
	5	V2,313		8	P1
13	1	Stevenson Papers	31	1	H1,145
	2	K3,98		2	W3,265
	3	P2,28	32	1	F1,153
	4	L3,201	34	1	W3,254
	5	S3,32		2	W3,24
	6	P2,124		3	W3,68
	6	M2,II,2	35	1	W3,60
14	1	P2		2	W3,104
15	1	H3,84	36	1	W3,183
	2	C6,104	37	1	W3,197
17	1	S3	38	1	W3,217
18	1	M2,II,36		2	K3,182
	2	H3,102		3	W3,228
19	1	M2,II,53		4	W3,234
	2	S3,135	39	1	W3,250
20	1	S3,190		2	W3,251
	2	S3,137		3	K1,2

REFERENCES

PAGE	REF. NO.	SOURCE	PAGE	REF. NO.	SOURCE
40	1	P2,163	57	6	W3,302
	2	W3,265	58	1	D2,113
	3	P2,154		2	D2,169
	4	W3,261	59	1	B3,296
	5	W3,265		2	K2,80
	6	W3,265		3	B3,330
	7	W3,264	62	1	R2,216
42	1	W3,268	63	1	R2,216
	2	S3,177	64	1	B1
	3	S3,180	65	1	B3,329
43	1	P2,155	66	1	U1
	2	K2,3	67	1	O1,42
	3	K3,180	69	1	S3,314
	4	B3,240		2	C3
44	1	W3,277	70	1	U1,505
	2	W3,273		2	M4
45	1	W3,277	71	1	S2
47	1	C4,227		2	S2
	2	B3	72	1	Die Hoëvelder
	3	K2,16			10 . 7 . 1964
48	1	K2,16		2	R1,74
	2	C4,276	73	1	G1,II, 148
	3	C4,278		2	W3,306
50	1	U1,502	74	1	W3,308
	2	W3,290	75	1	C4,336
	3	P2,163	76	1	W2,64
	4	D3,124	78	1	K3,190
51	1	P2,164		2	W3,308
	2	B4,31	79	1	S3,221
	3	B4,31	80	1	G1,149
	4	P2,65		2	C4,306
52	1	D3,127		3	C5,107
	2	M2,159	81	1	K2,69
	3	W3,295		2	W4,290
	3	D2,199		2	S3,221
53	1	W3,293		3	S2
	2	K1,14		4	C5,108
54	1	K2,49		5	S2
	1	M4	82	1	O1,50
	2	K1,14		2	G1,III,148
55	1	W3,297		3	S2
56	1	G1,II,130	83	1	K2,15
	2	D2,121		2	R2,215
57	1	D2,110		3	W3,309
	2	S3,208	84	1	W3,309
	2	W3,300	85	1	D2,192
	3	W3,300	86	1	W1,506
	4	M2,II,153	88	1	G1,II,151
	5	K3,185		2	G1,II,165

PAGE	REF. NO.	SOURCE	PAGE	REF. NO.	SOURCE
89	1	G1,II,165	113	4	C4
	2	A2,III,268	114	1	C2,3
	2	P2,181		2	K2,91
	3	P2,181		3	S1,77
90	1	S3,223		4	R1,81
	2	P2,181		5	D3,134
	3	M4	115	1	W4,302
91	1	O1,48		2	M4
	2	W3,314		3	D2,163
	3	O1,481	116	1	V2,332
92	1	W3,308		2	W4,303
93	1	A3,193		3	C3,57
94	1	S3,224		4	B3,35
95	1	S3,221	117	1	K2,92
96	1	W3,314		2	U1,507
97	1	C5,109	118	1	A2,III,302
	2	S3,224		2	G1,II,179
	3	W3,315		3	C4,349
	4	P2,186		4	B4,35
98	1	D2,146	119	1	W3,326
	2	D3,132		2	W3,326
100	1	W3,315		3	D3,133
102	1	B3,340		4	D2,169
	2	D2,152		4	W3,325
	3	O1,53		5	S3,228
	4	W3,320	120	1	S3,239
	5	B2,346		2	C4,341
103	1	P2,191		3	S3,234
	2	A2,III,288		4	W3,342
104	1	V2,331	121	1	K2,208
	2	O1,54		1	W3,330
105	1	S3,234		2	H3,213
	2	Stevenson Papers		3	H3,214
107	1	M1,II,398		4	L3,218
	2	G1,II,176	122	1	K3,24
108	1	D2,163		1	W3,334
	2	D2,161		2	W3,340
	3	M4		3	L3,219
	4	S2	123	1	W3,337
	5	S2		2	P2,203
	6	U1,505		3	A2,III,302
109	1	S2		4	P2,257
	2	D1		4	W3,341
110	1	K3,199		5	W3,343
	2	W3,319	124	1	W3,346
111	1	S3,234		2	S3,272
113	1	D2,162		3	H2,71
	2	D2,162		4	W3,368
	3	D1		5	S3,276

REFERENCES

PAGE	REF. NO.	SOURCE	PAGE	REF. NO.	SOURCE
125	1	S3,276	128	1	K3,512
	2	S3,279		2	L3,242
	3	W3,372		3	S3,280
	4	W3,372	129	1	S3,288
126	1	W3,376		2	A3,154
	2	W3,393		3	H3,280
	3	W3,401	130	1	W3,329
	4	W3,393		1	A2,III,305
	4	W3,407	131	1	A3,118
127	1	W3,401	135	1	D3,135

INDEX